The English Cricketers' Trip

CARPENTER CAFFYN LOCKYER STEPHENSON PARR GRUNDY CAESAR HAYWARD

WISDEN DIVER JOHN LILLYWHITE JACKSON

Taken on board ship at Liverpool, September 7th 1859

The English Cricketers' Trip

to Canada and the United States in 1859

FRED. LILLYWHITE

Introduction by

Robin Marlar

World's Work Ltd.

First published by Fred Lillywhite in 1860
This edition published by World's Work Ltd
The Windmill Press, Kingswood, Tadworth, Surrey
Printed in Great Britain by
William Clowes (Beccles) Ltd, Beccles & London
SBN 437 08930 4

Introduction
by Robin Marlar

This is the first, and perhaps the most interesting, of all the books about cricket tours. It was written by Fred Lillywhite, third son of William, the great round-arm bowler of Sussex, the Nonpareil himself. Fred Lillywhite was 27 when first he began to think about a cricketing expedition overseas—not to Australia as we would nowadays assume, but to Canada and the United States. Cricket had been played there by the founding fathers of Virginia and the Carolinas 200 years before this tour. Fred Lillywhite eventually organised and negotiated the tour, bringing together the arch-rivals, George Parr, William Clarke's successor as leader of the famous All-England Eleven, who captained this touring team, and John Wisden, founder of the United All-England Eleven, the equally famous splinter group.

For once truly united, together they were able to pick so many of the best professionals of that generation. They chose six from each of the two professional Elevens, four from Surrey, three from Notts and Cambridge and two from Sussex. This was a fair reflection of current strength. Edgar Willsher of Kent, certainly, was missing, and would have made John Jackson a formidable partner with his fast left-handers, but not many others qualified ahead of this company. No wonder they were successful against relatively weak opponents, even at twice the numerical strength. They were, all of them, cricketing giants, daily players, daily-bread players, professionals, among the first professional independent sportsmen anywhere in the world.

Such was the towering nature of their skill that they could not only force the establishment to change the Laws—about bowling, for instance—but they so spread knowledge of cricket that the game became part of the lore and custom of England. Just as Mynn and Pilch and Felix and old Lillywhite, father of these two tourists, built the platform, so did the younger men create the international sporting plinth on which the statuesque figure of the mighty Doctor, W. G. Grace himself, would eventually stand.

Did Fred Lillywhite know that he was prompter for a group of pioneers, the man both promoting and chronicling the start of a great tradition? Either way, he did not live long enough to see it established.

Some of the party, like the ironically-named Julius Caesar, certainly never thought of themselves as brave adventurers. Yet there is so much gallantry about Lillywhite's own persistence, and his players' faith in his arrangements. It shows in the fact that the team of professionals settled financially for less than they had asked for three years before. Perhaps some felt that time was running out. By 1859, only three were under 30, and only seven of the 13 were to reach 50. Death came early to the mid-Victorians.

Fred Lillywhite's qualities show in his desire to make a proper job of the tour, to demonstrate to the Canadians and Americans the best possible presentation of English cricket, from the proper advertising of the matches right down to the inclusion on the scorecard of the latest wicket to fall. Hence his pre-occupation with the transport of his precious printing press, and his irritation with those who cursed his paraphernalia. At one stage George Parr consigned both Fred and his tent to "an unmentionable region". Between Buffalo, New York, and Hamilton, Ontario, the entire contraption was lost, and so there were no scorecards at all. Perhaps Fred was right in his insistence on the players' helping as porters. This has been a recurring theme with baggage-masters ever since.

His qualities are seen, too, in his willingness to take a chance with wind and weather on sea and on land. Few of the party could have known what to expect on a voyage through the autumn gales of the North Atlantic on the long but tiny new-fangled sail-and-steam ships, with their unreliable engines. Once there, the team may have admired the spectacular colours of the North American fall, but by October the pinch of winter was upon the land. Cricket in the snow is no fun at all. George Parr had every excuse for calling for his "hot gin and water".

Fred Lillywhite writes in a style which reads easily 120 years later. He had had some practice as the compiler of The Guide to Cricketers, and the 13th edition covers the tour. Fred's own review of the season was akin to the Editor's Notes in Wisden today, and often landed him in hot water (and no gin) with the powers that were, notably MCC: the first issue of Wisden's Almanack, without such notes, did not appear until 1864. Lillywhite's story of his trip, while similar in many ways to Wickets In The West, the R. A. Fitzgerald account of the tour the amateurs made in 1872, is more direct in its style than the erudite prose of the classically-educated Fitzgerald.

Fred Lillywhite was a worker; writing, selling, making, dispatching his books and his cricket equipment must have been a lonely and arduous task for a man whom others found difficult. When this book was published, he had only six years to live.

Finally, though every detail is different, it is astonishing that so little has changed about the moods of a major cricket tour abroad. The impressions of the start, the voyage of discovery, the warmth of the welcome, give way to a familiar sense of righteous indignation at later treatment by the hosts which falls short of the high standards to which the party have grown accustomed. Cricketers can be a spoilt breed.

Then comes criticism by the press, as represented by Fred Lillywhite himself, of the twin powers within the team, Parr and Wisden, who not only failed to help themselves on tour, but also failed to help him on their safe return. By then most of the troubles had been forgotten amid the euphoric reception accorded to the conquering heroes. At the celebration dinner in old Godalming, one of the cradles of Surrey cricket, all the pain and problems are forgotten until Julius Caesar puts his feet in it, at least according to the gospel of Fred Lillywhite.

How familiar it all is! How grateful we are for these hints of the passions which mutedly raged within this group of great cricketers from the game's Middle Ages. Sadly we know too little of most of them, but it is worth setting down some of the details of their lives before and after they were changed by this, their two-month trip as cricketing pioneers.

ROBIN MARLAR

July 1980

FRED LILLYWHITE

Born July 7, 1829 at Hove, Sussex
Age on tour 30
37 at his death on September 15, 1866

"This name", he wrote of himself in the ninth edition of The Guide to Cricketers, published in 1856, "may not appear correctly classed under the head of 'Professionals of England' but being closely connected with them in many matters, can perhaps claim the privilege." At that time, and for years, he was pre-occupied with the authoritative historical work, Scores and Biographies, dating from 1772. The estimate for printing was then £500, a huge sum for him to find. Notice that the 12 players, guaranteed £600, finally received no less than £1,080 between them, more than twice as much as the cost to him of what had become his life's work. Caffyn, at least, was pleased with his £90.

Lillywhite was said not to be the most reliable of chroniclers, and G. D. Martineau gives Arthur Haygarth the credit for compiling Scores and Biographies. Eventually Fred Lillywhite fell foul of the MCC Committee, who had hitherto supported his guide, and in 1865 they withdrew their patronage because he had "exceeded the fair limits of criticism upon cricketers," a charge which has a thoroughly 20th-century ring about it. Fred Lillywhite was then charged by the secretary over damage to a printing press. He was a man who clearly had too much to do. He had gone into partnership with John Wisden at 2 New Coventry Street, Leicester Square—not far from the present Lillywhites—in 1855 but that partnership split after this tour.

Thereafter he was based at The Oval, where he was not only a cricket outfitter, supplying cricket clothes, prints and photographs, but he also sold croquet sets for up to five guineas, and sponsored such novel devices as "the patent portable hand-watering engine, the best invention ever produced for making a good wicket (so desirable) and watering a garden, or even washing carriages or decks of ships." On the latter subject he had, after this historic tour, become something of an expert.

GEORGE PARR

Born May 22, 1826 at Radcliffe-on-Trent, Notts
Age on tour 33
65 at his death on June 23, 1891
All-England Eleven

George Parr, captain of the All-England Eleven, of Notts and of touring teams to North America and Australia, lived and died in the glorious ivy-covered Old Manor House in the village where he was born. His family had been gentleman farmers on the same land for two centuries. For this reason, George Parr always considered himself a cut above the other professionals. In skill with bat and ball, in cricket wisdom, he could well claim to be.

He was 19 when he played his first match at Lord's. He made his start with Clarke's All-England Eleven in 1847 when, in successive matches, he hit 100 at Leicester, 78 not out at York and 64 at Manchester—all against 18 or more in the field. We tend to forget how much more difficult batting was in matches against odds, with an over-crowded field. Thick-set, blue-eyed and often grumpy, Parr was especially apt to become tetchy when nature played up, whether on a stagecoach, in a thunderstorm, or on board ship. Then he needed his gin and water. On a later trip to New Zealand he was, as captain, expected to kiss the Queen of the Maoris. He called up Jackson and said: "You're a gypsy—you do it." Jackson refused, so Parr kissed the old lady, whereupon she gave him a gem stone, telling him that as long as he kept it in his pocket he would never have to work. And he never did. Perhaps he really kept it in the battered hat-box he carried around with him for many years, and about which Richard Daft, his successor as captain of the AEE, used to wig him without ever discovering the secret of its contents.

Once, on a rough night in Cornwall, an old farmer—"as deaf as an adder" according to Daft—pointed a blunderbuss at Parr's head before ever the players of the AEE could ask for food and shelter. That was the night Jackson got a lather of cream from the dairy all over his whiskers. Although Parr tended to crouch at the wicket, and thus took a battering on his hands, he refused to offer only a dead-bat defence, and was thus able to play his sweep to leg, his own special shot. At this he excelled to such an extent that a tree on that boundary at Trent Bridge was named after him. One of its branches was buried with him.

Richard Daft writes of Parr with affection, telling another story of the Lion of the North at a boxing match in Derby where, as the ring of men surged, he kept backing away from the combatants until he disappeared through a door and down a flight of stairs, his fall broken by a stack of churchwarden pipes. When he died eight months after marrying his housekeeper, he was a sad and gouty shadow of the man who had kept the All-England Eleven just ahead of its rival United Eleven in the toughest of all contemporary matches, the fixture between professional teams that, more than any other, proclaimed northern supremacy.

JULIUS CAESAR

Born March 25, 1830 at Godalming, Surrey
Age on tour 29
47 at his death on March 6, 1878
All-England Eleven

A splendid batsman, severe on bowling below the best. He hit hard and cleanly for a man of only 5ft 7in. His physique was strong—"a big man in a little room," Caffyn called him. Although he was a noted boxer, he was an exceedingly nervous character who would not sleep by himself. He thought disaster inevitable, fearing that the hotel would be burnt down during the night. At Hereford he once woke the entire household up by ringing a bell and shouting "fire!" after waking up and hearing a reveller on his way home. He thought he should be dropped after each low score—another example of a modern behavioural pattern. He was a noted shot, but went to his death remembering how he had accidentally killed a gamekeeper.

In his young days it was possible for the family to field a whole team of Surrey Caesars. One story of Caesar on tour Lillywhite does not tell. In New York he found a bar where London porter was on tap. Well in their cups, Caesar and an American had an argument which the Yankee settled by pointing a revolver at Caesar's nose saying: "This is my card." Next morning Caesar told his teammates that he was going to give the first American he met in Britain a hiding, "even if I get three months for it".

He was on the umpires' list in his later years, which must have been saddened by the death of his son, a professional at Charterhouse, at the age of 21. The body of Julius Jnr. was found on the railway line between Guildford and Godalming on October 3, 1876.

WILLIAM CAFFYN

Born February 2, 1828 at Reigate, Surrey
Age on tour 31
91 at his death on August 28, 1919
United All-England Eleven

William Caffyn has given us, in his "ghosted" autobiography*, the only other significant account of the first overseas cricket tour. How appropriate that it should be his. Despite his dislike of the sea Caffyn, small and neat, was a member of the first three English touring sides, for he also went twice to Australia, first with Stephenson and then with Parr. At the end of Parr's tour, he stayed in Australia and there became, in both Melbourne and Sydney, the coach largely responsible for laying the foundations of the great Australian sides that were to prove themselves capable of beating England in the Age of Grace.

He learned his cricket at Reigate Grammar School. His father was a barber—and the local bandmaster. In due course, William and his wife were to earn a living in Australia and England as hairdressers. His uncle Walter once kept wicket for Surrey, so there was cricket in the family. William made his first appearance at The Oval in 1849 at the age of 21, and from there he went into Clarke's All-England Eleven, joining the breakaway with Wisden, Dean and the rest of the rebels in 1852. He was the most elegant batsman of his generation, and almost certainly the finest cutter the game had yet known. His batting was a pleasure to watch, especially on a good wicket, even for opponents with knowledgeable appreciation like Richard Daft. His figures show him to be one of the "cracks". He was also Surrey's leading bowler in a round-arm style which we today call that of a medium-pacer. He was in his prime between 1857 and 1863. One of his contemporaries thought that the more runs he made the better he bowled.

He hated batting on rough wickets, such as Lord's, where he struggled, sometimes successfully, against Jackson, and the story is told of his leaving the ground at Sheffield after a deluge, only to be brought back with his bag "by some ruffians" demanding more cricket for their threepence. "It was so wet that water spluttered in

**71 Not Out, written by R. P. Daft, son of Richard Daft, Parr's successor, who played once for Notts and wrote on cricket as Mid-On.*

your face as you fielded the ball," according to another Surrey player.

He came back from Australia in 1871, played in only three more Surrey matches in 1872 and 1873, and then retired from first-class cricket. His bowling was not so effective on the better wickets then prepared. Afterwards, he took coaching jobs at several schools, including Eton. The last was Haileybury, and so it was in Hertford that he settled and once again took up hairdressing. Drawn matches and pitches that were too good upset him as the century turned and he wrote down his enchanting and informative story. Caffyn still had almost a score of years left, during which Surrey paid him an annuity of £39, for he never had a benefit. Thus he outlived all the other tourists, having led perhaps the fullest life of them all.

ROBERT CARPENTER

Born November 18, 1830 at Cambridge
Age on tour 28
70 at his death on July 13, 1901
United All-England Eleven

Like Hayward, the name of Carpenter was perpetuated. His son Bob, christened Herbert, the youngest of his large Victorian family of nine, for years helped to keep Essex, then a relatively weak county, in first-class company. Robert Carpenter was 27 before he played at Lord's for the first time; he made 45, mostly off Jackson's thunderbolts, for the United against the All-England Eleven. He was known as the champion back player of the century. But he went down the wicket to spin bowling, as well. A brilliant fielder, he was often at point with Hayward at cover-point behind him. They lured inexperienced batsmen into attempting runs. Carpenter let the ball go, and Hayward threw the unwary runner out.

Like Grundy and Diver, Carpenter was an after-dinner entertainer whose songs and ditties were much in demand. He was another member of the party who kept up his association with cricket through coaching. He was at Marlborough where, according to James Pycroft, he taught the boys to cut without moving the right foot. He also umpired in the big matches.

ALFRED JOHN "DUCKY" DIVER

Born July 6, 1824 at Cambridge
Age on tour 35
51 at his death on March 25, 1876
All-England Eleven

Diver, like Grundy, was older than the other members of the party. He features, along with Parr and other stalwarts of the previous generation, as one of the subjects of Anderson's sketches at Lord's. He was most famous as a long-stop, a position in the field of greater significance then than later because of the bumpiness of the pitches. Long-stop was not only required to take balls which bounced over batsmen and wicket keeper, he was also expected to cover a wide track of the field on both off-side and leg-side. Furthermore, it was his job to prevent single byes being taken by the sheer speed of his pick-up and return. At all of this Diver excelled: in addition, he was a fine batsman and a useful bowler in two styles—fast with round-arm action and slow with lobs. Positioned at long-stop—at both ends—he became an excellent judge of the game, so much so that George Parr, his regular captain, often took his cue from Diver's opinion of a bowler.

Apart from his key role in the AEE, he played also for Cambridgeshire (then very strong, with Carpenter and Hayward to bat, and Buttress, the cricketing ventriloquist, to bowl) and once in 1858 for Nottinghamshire. Subsequently he became an excellent coach at Rugby School. His nephew, Edwin James Diver, played for Surrey and Warwickshire, and for both Gentlemen and Players.

JAMES OR JEMMY GRUNDY

Born March 5, 1824 at New Retford, Notts
Age on tour 35
49 at his death on November 24, 1873
United All-England Eleven

A superbly accurate bowler who could "land 'em on a cheese-plate" for hour upon hour. A good defensive player with the bat, and sound anywhere in the field. He was, by a few months, the oldest member of the party. His method of bowling was persistent length and direction, and in 1854 he took no fewer than 196 wickets, for under five runs apiece. When teammates suggested he give batsmen one to hit, he would always demur: "Nay, I shall give him a good 'un. If he wants to hit me, let him come and do it."

He went to Lord's in 1851, and was on the bowling staff there for many years; always, it seems, a man "neatly turned out". His prowess as a songster was famous among his fellows. They gradually came to respect his batting, too; especially after he had scored an important century in six-and-a-half hours, his one and only three-figure innings.

TOM HAYWARD

Born March 21, 1835 at Chatteris, Cambridgeshire
Age on tour 34
41 at his death on July 21, 1876
All-England Eleven

A member of a famous Cambridge cricketing family, Tom was the brother of Daniel Hayward, who was for many years in charge of the ground at Fenner's, even then established as one of the finest cricket fields in England. He was the uncle of "young" Tom, who later became such a stalwart at Surrey and was himself the precursor of another young man born in Cambridge who went to The Oval, John Berry, later Sir Jack, Hobbs. Old Tom Hayward himself had a graceful style, with a fine flourish to his defence. He was a good onside player who used his wrists to drop a rising ball or stop a shooter, of which there were many. Essentially he was a half-forward player, as many modern batsmen are.

Like a famous modern, Denis Compton, he was also one of the worst judges of a run, and responsible for running out many a partner. Of all the early deaths among members of this party, Hayward's is perhaps the least surprising, for he was always "of delicate health", which usually indicated a weak chest, or "consumption", as tuberculosis was then called.

JOHN JACKSON

Born May 21, 1833 at Bungay, Suffolk
Age on tour 26
68 at his death on November 4, 1901
All-England Eleven

A week after John's birth, the Jackson family were back in Nottinghamshire. It was to Ollerton that England's first terrorising fast bowler always claimed to belong. Known in his early days as Jem Crow, Jackson was paid sixpence an hour as a teenager to field and bowl at Southwell, seven miles from home. By 1855, William Clarke selected this 14-stone six-footer for his North and All-England Elevens. Off a run of four or five yards, and with a round-arm action, he was for years the fastest bowler in England. Like many a fast bowler since, he would drink almost anything, from a bowl of chilled cream in Cornwall, to the rum meant to disinfect a nose broken in the nets at Cambridge.

With Tinley's slow lobs at the other end, Jackson wreaked havoc among the provincial sides of 18 and 22 against whom the experts played. "What chance does a man have with a thunderbolt at one end and a corkscrew at the other?" someone asked. It was open chat among the professionals that he was too quick for the likes of Grundy, whom he once made "stamp and swear like a lunatic" after he had been hit. Even Caffyn found his pace too hot, especially on the bad wicket at Lord's. After every wicket that he took, Jackson blew his nose so loudly that Robert Carpenter nicknamed him Foghorn.

He always took his pay in gold, and when his trousers burst from the sheer weight of sovereigns, everyone had to stand back whilst he picked up his wages. Like many of his type since, he hated batsmen to hit his bowling. Some say he invented the bouncer. Once, after C. I. Thornton had slogged him out of the ground, he shouted: "Oh, to hell with that kind of batting!" It is said that one unknown, but suffering, batsman left the crease after being hit on the ankle by a ball from Jackson, only to be told he was not out: "Maybe I am, maybe I ain't, but I'm going all the same," was his answer. Asked whether he had ever taken all 10 wickets, he replied: "No, but for North against South I got nine and lamed Johnny Wisden so that he could not bat. That was as good as ten, eh?" Mostly he made the ball leave the bat, but Dr. E. M. Grace averred that he could move it both ways.

In 1866, he fell while fielding in the Notts game against Yorkshire, broke a blood vessel behind the knee, was out of action for 20 weeks and never again played for the county, though he did appear for the AEE in 1867. By then Wootton and Shaw were bowling for Notts. A benefit in 1874 raised some £300. Eventually he became caterer, groundsman and bowler in Liverpool. Thereafter, the road was downhill. He took a job as a warehouseman, received 5s 6d a week from the Cricketers' Fund until, as the third oldest of this touring party, he died in the Liverpool Workhouse Infirmary. His friends had a whip round to raise enough to give him a decent burial.

JOHN LILLYWHITE

Born November 10, 1826 at Hove, Sussex
Age on tour 32
47 at his death on October 27, 1874
United All-England Eleven

The eldest of this generation of Lillywhites, John was an admirable batsman with a sound defence and the ability to drive well. A useful change bowler known in cricket as the "mud bowler," he also excelled at cover-point. Like his father, the great bowler, the Nonpareil, he was a short, square, strongly-built man, and for a few seasons one of the very best. However, according to Caffyn his eyesight faded early, though it was clear enough for him to score a century against Surrey, including Caffyn, in 1863, when he was 36.

John Lillywhite also featured in the historic no-balling incident that ultimately led to the legalising of over-arm bowling. In the Surrey v England match at The Oval in 1862, John Lillywhite no-balled Edgar Willsher six times in succession, and it was rumoured in the North that he had been engaged as umpire for the purpose. Next day, the England players refused to take the field unless John Lillywhite was removed. He was. Lillywhite had a rehearsal for this drama on the tour, for he no-balled the American opening bowler in New York. Willsher and Lillywhite fell out over this episode, but only temporarily. In the sense that the bowling Law was rewritten two years later to legalise the free-swinging action many had already adopted illegally and by stealth, this can be seen as the last great contribution of the Lillywhite family on the field of play.

Like his brothers, James and Fred, he went into business as a supplier of cricket goods. His premises were in Euston Road, London, and this business was the precursor of the modern Lillywhites. His brother James's operation began at Cheltenham, where James was coach, and became Lillywhite Frowd, another business which survived.

TOM LOCKYER

Born November 1, 1826 at Croydon, Surrey
Age on tour 32
43 at his death on December 22, 1869
United All-England Eleven

Acknowledged by his peers to be the finest wicketkeeper of his generation in England, on this tour Lockyer gave free rein to his skill and speed to the delight of spectators who, perhaps, did not understand his role too well. What made him exceptional was his use of the left hand to gather legside balls which most contemporary 'keepers were wont to let go through to the long-stop. Unlike many of his rivals, he was happy taking bowlers fast and slow.

It is important to visualise the state of the pitches, both in England and North America, and the fields that had to be set. Apart from The Oval and Fenner's, most pitches were rough, even though Thomas Lord moved the turf as he moved his ground. The implements for caring for it were rudimentary, and groundsmanship primitive. It was *de rigeur* for a wicketkeeper to stand close to the stumps. Hence the importance of the long-stop some 30 yards behind him.

Like many other 'keepers, Lockyer had an odd temperament and some curious clothes, notably an old waistcoat with sleeves which he wore for years. He may also have been the first 'keeper to guard against a finger injury with a stall made like a thimble, a common enough protection in modern gloves. A loose-limbed six-footer, he was a fine hitter, never knew when he was beaten and was an all-round cricketer well able to take off his gloves and bowl fast round-arm.

HEATHFIELD HARMAN STEVENSON

Born April 3, 1833 at Esher, Surrey
Age on tour 26
63 at his death on December 17, 1896
All-England Eleven

An historic figure: the first man to captain an England team in Australia—on the highly successful tour sponsored by the catering company, Spiers and Pond, in 1861. He was a tall man, and as such a strong-driving batsman. Like so many big men who have followed him, he was no cutter. He was also a fine fast-medium bowler with a pronounced break-back because of an unusual action. He was second only to Lockyer as a wicketkeeper in his generation, and kept in many of the AEE matches, Lockyer of the United being among the opposition. However, Stevenson made his reputation as a bowler, and for four years was almost unique in his ability to break the ball back with a round-arm action. Eventually his fingers lost their snap.

He was given the nickname Spurgeon by George Parr because he always wore a black frock coat, and his distinctive physical feature was a thumb which he could put out at will. He would tease his teammates with the trick. Caesar hated to watch it. Eventually Stevenson joined Caesar on the umpires' list. In 1884, as a distinguished elder statesman among the professionals, he spoke out against the increase of throwing, which led to a change in the Law which curbed the abuse for a decade. Nor was this all he achieved. He was a great coach at Uppingham in the early 1870s. The Cambridge Eleven of 1877 contained no fewer than five of his protégés—an astonishing and unrepeated proportion.

JOHN WISDEN

Born October 5, 1826 at Brighton, Sussex
Age on tour 32
57 at his death on April 5, 1884
United All-England Eleven

The Little Wonder, as he was known, was a tiny man, only 5ft 4½in tall and weighing 7st in his prime. John Wisden was the son of a builder who went to live with, and learned his cricket from, Tom Box, the famous Sussex wicketkeeper, who kept the Hanover Arms in Brighton and gave Wisden—"a little six-penn'th of coppers"—a job as a pot boy. An all-rounder who hit centuries—not so common in those days—against Kent and Yorkshire, he played for Sussex from 1845 to 1863, and was most famous as a bowler of "fast and ripping" off-breaks, especially after taking all 10 South wickets, and all clean-bowled, as "given man" for the North in 1850.

At that time he was the joint owner with Parr of a ground at Leamington. He averaged 225 wickets a year over 12 seasons. In 1852, with James Dean, he founded the United All-England Eleven. Three years later he entered a partnership in the cricket and cigar business with Frederick Lillywhite. That partnership, as we can tell from hints provided by the advertisements in the book, may never have recovered from this tour. In 1857 he became the secretary of the Cricketers' Fund Friendly Society, whose assets depended largely on the proceeds of the great match, an annual event, between the All-England and the United. Wisden held that position until his death.

In 1864, John Wisden's Cricketer's Almanack appeared as just another cricket annual. The first issue of the cricketer's bible has since proved a worthwhile investment. Issued at a shilling, which was still the price in 1915, plus a penny postage, copies now change hands at up to £500. Wisden clearly was determined to learn from Lillywhite's unpopularity at Lord's. In the edition of 1866 it is stated that: "John Wisden & Co. have avoided making remarks upon the play or players". For the first six issues there was no writing at all, merely a record of the matches. Wisden was, like Stevenson, a great coach, and for the three years he was engaged at Harrow School, Eton were never victorious at Lord's.

LOCKYER AT THE WICKET.

THE ENGLISH CRICKETERS TRIP TO CANADA AND THE UNITED STATES

BY

FRED LILLYWHITE.

THE

ENGLISH CRICKETERS'

TRIP TO CANADA

AND

THE UNITED STATES.

BY FRED. LILLYWHITE.

LONDON:

F. LILLYWHITE, 15, KENNINGTON OVAL, S.; KENT & CO.,

23, PATERNOSTER ROW, E.C.

1860.

JOHN SUCH, PRINTER, BUDGE ROW, WATLING STREET, CITY.

THE
ENGLISH CRICKETERS' TRIP
TO
CANADA
AND
THE UNITED STATES.

PREFACE.

In offering to the kindly notice of the British public the following narrative, derived from personal association, of the recent trip to America of the Twelve English Cricketers, the writer ventures to bespeak a generous indulgence to the few remarks with which he desires to introduce this record of their adventures and their exploits.

It has happened to have been the lot and privilege of the writer of these pages to have attended, professionally, the earliest wanderings of the Eleven of England throughout the length and breadth of the United Kingdom, and it has ever been his earnest endeavour, in the discharge of his duties, whilst chronicling their performances in the tented field, to disseminate amongst all classes that love of "England's pastime," to which its manly and health-bestowing qualities so justly, and so naturally entitle it.

To have left no record, therefore, of so novel an occurrence as this memorable expedition would, the writer feels, have been a subject for universal regret, and however deeply he is sensible of his own short comings, in attempting a task which, indeed, requires the exercise of a far abler pen than his, he is not without hope that the favourable consideration of his readers will be accorded to his humble attempt to fulfil the duty which he has undertaken.

That kind forbearance has been too often granted to the writer, not to lead him to the cheerful anticipation that his labours will not have been altogether fruitless; and that his object in appearing thus prominently before the public, will be fully recognised in an eager desire to promote and extend, even further than it has already prevailed, that love for the noble game of Cricket, which has been of such inestimable value to all communities where it has been practised.

F. L.

LIST OF ILLUSTRATIONS.

THE

ENGLISH CRICKETERS' TRIP

TO

CANADA & THE UNITED STATES.

On the Evening of September 6, 1859, Twelve Cricketers of England met at the George Hotel, Liverpool, to be in readiness to embark for Quebec the following morning, per the "Montreal Ocean Steam-ship Company's ship *Novia Scotian*, Captain Borland." The Twelve comprised Caffyn, Lockyer, H. H. Stephenson, Julius Cæsar, (Surrey), G. Parr, Grundy, Jackson (Nottingham), Wisden, John Lillywhite, (Sussex), Carpenter, T. Hayward, Diver, (Cambridge); to these was added Fred. Lillywhite, who, with his tent, press, &c. accompanied the expedition in his professional capacity of reporter of the matches to be played across the water. The next morning, the 7th September, the whole party proceeded to the ship, which was anchored off Liverpool docks.

Before proceeding to describe what occurred from the time the anchor was weighed, it may not be out of place to inform the reader *how* these Cricketers became so "domiciled" on board of the said ship—the *Novia Scotian*.

Their preparations were hastily made, and indeed were not concluded until the middle of August, during the grand week at Canterbury, when Mr. Wilder, the President of the Cricketer's Fund, was in a position to announce to the parties interested that Mr. Pickering, of Montreal, (whom most of our readers will remember as the celebrated "Field"), had agreed to the proposal which, with the consent of the Twelve Players, Mr. Wilder had made for their remuneration. As far back as 1856, a correspondence took place between Messrs. W. P. Pickering, Montreal, R. Waller, New York, and Fred. Lillywhite, London, respecting certain matches to be played in Canada and the States, but owing to the terms asked, just double what they received for this trip, coupled with other circumstances, such as the playing ground, &c., arrangements could not then be entered into. The American panic then intervened, but, as soon as it had subsided, and the " dollars " were again in free circulation, the correspondence was renewed between Messrs. Pickering and Waller, and owing to the former being so intimately known to Mr. Wilder, in London, a correspondence took place between these two gentlemen, and ultimately by *private interviews with the players themselves,* Mr. Wilder became security, on behalf of Mr. Pickering, for the Twelve to receive £50 each, and to have all their expenses paid, from the time of their departure from, and return to, Liverpool. Previously to Mr. Wilder becoming responsible, Mr. Pickering had secured a sum of £500 through Mr. Waller, for two matches in the States, viz., New York and Philadelphia, and also £250 from Hamilton, Upper Canada.

Some doubt having arisen, in the public mind, as to whom the credit of getting the English across the Atlantic should be attributed, caused the following letter from Parr and Wisden to be published in *Bell's Life in London*, January 8, 1860.

" Mr. Editor,—As there appears to be a good deal of doubt respecting the parties by whom we were engaged in our late Transatlantic trip, we beg to inform you that our engagement to play the four matches was made solely with the Montreal Cricket Club, of Lower Canada, whose guarantee we accepted for our expenses and remuneration, and that we had nothing whatever to do with the States, or any one else, in the matter.—Yours, &c.

" George Parr,
" John Wisden."

Mr. Pickering, on behalf of the Montreal Club, therefore, received £750, and had to conduct the English party throughout their travels, paying all expenses, and, when they were about to return to England from Quebec, the Montreal gentlemen had to make up a balance of something more than £100, which, however, we believe, has been now almost all collected. Such is the origin of these international contests, which received the most substantial assistance from the gentlemen in the States.

THE NOVA SCOTIAN LEAVING THE MERSEY.

THE START

from the Docks was made at half past two o'clock, on Wednesday, the 7th, per tug, to the ship anchored in the Mersey. The owners had contracted to convey the English party to and fro. Passengers arrived on board just before three o'clock, and the opposite engraving represents the departure. The tug conveyed a vast number of cricketers and supporters of the game in Liverpool, who gave three hearty English cheers for the success of their countrymen.

At 4.15 the anchor was weighed, the sailors timing their labours to a popular and nautical ditty, the words of which were about as follows:

"Here's success to the old black-jack
"Whisky, jolly;
"And may we all get plenty of that
"Whisky, boys—ho—jolly."

The melody came to a premature close, and the good ship was then fairly on her way to Quebec. We soon arrived at the acknowledged starting point from England, where the firing of a gun announced the same. Passed the Isle of Man at 10.45, seventy-five miles distant from Liverpool, and all retired to rest; the only one who had selected a spot for his future accommodation, in case it might be required, was John Lillywhite, and this was immediately behind the wheel. The morning of

THURSDAY, September 8,

was lovely. Most of the cricketers were on deck at six o'clock. The sea was calm with a fresh and favourable breeze; we were off the Irish coast, going at the rate of eleven knots an hour. At twelve o'clock a.m. we were distant from Liverpool 220 miles. At this period a heavy sea sprung up, with a head wind, which reduced our "going" from eleven to five knots an hour. Stephenson, Caffyn, John Lillywhite, and Jackson were not quite so comfortable as when on land, and were frequently evincing their arithmetical propensities, by casting up their accounts, the balancing of which they found to be a most troublesome and unpleasant operation.

Our places having been secured, both for berths and meals, those who were well now began to " look up," the officers of the ship, and we very soon found that we had a jolly lot to deal with, which increased our confidence, and made us, at once, *sailors*. Our first conversation with Captain Borland raised him high in our estimation as a good hearted, thoroughly courageous, experienced and weather-beaten sailor. His expressions gave us reason to think that he would make every one present comfortable, if possible. Some of the cricketers, however, *thought* that unless he could prevent the ship from rolling about, his attempts to secure our comfort would not be attended with very great success. We received many indulgences, and much valuable information from Mr. McDonald, the first mate, whose eye was sure to be where anything might be going wrong, and the seamanlike manner in which he gave his commands, procured for him the ready obedience and respect of all the sailors. Then we had the excellent attention of the purser, Mr. Jenkins, who apparently could not do too much to oblige us. The chief engineer also is a gentleman of great eminence in his profession, so that we felt no doubt about our safe arrival at Quebec. The kindness and attention of Mr. Jones, the second mate, was also particularly noticed by the English cricketers; in fact, the whole of the officers and crew, down to the captain's boy, Jack, were as pleasant a ship's company as one could possibly wish to sail with. We had now ascertained the exact time for meals, and, with the exception of those whose stomachs would not allow them to "devour," all attended to the sound of the bell. Breakfast at half past eight, at which there was no lack of *rolls*, lunch at twelve, dinner at four, tea at seven, and supper from nine to eleven. It was about four, p.m., this day, Thursday, that the shores of Ireland were fast lessening in the distance; the sky was no longer blue, and the waves began to get *very* " bumpy," so much so, as Wisden remarked, " as to require the immediate use of the roller," upon which some one said, " there were always plenty of rollers on the sea shore." Among those at this period who were particularly noticed to be labouring under disagreeable heaviness were John Lillywhite, at the wheel, Caffyn, Stephenson and Jackson in their bunks. At 4.30, p.m., we had the

SHIP IN A HEAVY GALE.

last look at land through the captain's glass, and then ascertained that we should have 1600 miles more to accomplish ere we should again have the pleasure of a similar sight. The captain here ordered more sail up, as the "wind was drawing aft a little." There was not anything like the number of passengers at dinner, as on the previous day, when in the Mersey, no doubt from the fact that they could not relish food under the circumstances. Among the English party, who took possession of the seats allotted to them, were Hayward, Carpenter, Parr, Wisden, Lockyer, Cæsar, Grundy, and Fred. Lillywhite, and most of these did not remain long, as the ship began to roll fearfully. Later in the evening the breeze freshened almost into a gale, and the quicksilver in the barometer fell rapidly. Upon casting one's eye round the deck, the usual places were filled by those to whom a sea voyage was anything but one of pleasure, and these appeared exceedingly desirous of putting foot on land again. Upon turning round you would find two or three passengers on their backs, an excellent position, when the ship takes a severe roll. Caffyn and Stephenson here attempted the task of going below, when an alarming pitch at the moment caused them both to be precipitated to the bottom of the steps, and nothing more was seen of them for two days and a half. At this moment, too, Lockyer, who had up to this period been perfectly well, very good naturedly enquired of Grundy, "how he liked the motion," to which question, he could get no answer, but a sigh, his heart and stomach being too full for utterance, except in one peculiar way. A rubber at whist, among those who were well, finished the night, and most were at rest at half-past nine o'clock.

FRIDAY, September 9.

Shortly after five o'clock, a.m., all sails were hauled in, the boatswain's whistle being heard all over the ship. The equinoctial gales had evidently set in, of which the breakfast seats, at half-past eight o'clock, gave ample proof. "Oh! a mere cat's-paw," says the chief officer. "Oh! thankee," replied Lockyer, exerting, among others, his very utmost to keep on his legs. The gale increased, and we were in the midst of a hurricane. Some half of the passengers did not leave their berths, and the head-aches were numerous and violent—one passenger especially, a Frenchman, who had No. 81, a berth above Fred. Lillywhite, did not leave it for sixty-five hours. In the depth of his distress the poor fellow kept shouting " stew-hart," although that functionary's hands were too full to attend to him immediately. Owing to the novelty of the situation, the groaning of some, the splash and thump of the waves against the sides of the ship, the howling of the wind, the flapping of the sails, and the incessant tramp of feet upon deck, sleep was quite out of the question; so there lay the unfortunate foreigner, with nothing to keep breath in his body, but warm water and sugar, a very poor sweetener in his cup of bitter annoyances. After his sixty-five hours rest, he attempted to land himself on the floor of the berth, endeavouring, first, to get a footing on the side of his fellow passenger's bunk, but, in so doing, the brass railings, on which he entirely depended for his safe landing gave way, and he was prostrated on the spot he had so industriously endeavoured to make; he was, consequently, rolled about and bruised, until the " stewhart," which word he could only just utter, could make his appearance. Parr and Wisden were immediately opposite, and having heard the poor fellow's groaning, and the laughing of his partner, which could not be restrained, were witnesses of the sight that presented itself. Owing to the fearful pitching of the ship, Fred. Lillywhite could render no other assistance than to " wake up " the steward, who " Monsieur," was now totally unable to call for. The " moving tale " had to be related regularly shortly before lunch, the poor Frenchman, with the warm water and sugar, being anxiously enquired after by other passengers, as well as by the Cricketers. One more circumstance occurred; after so lengthened a confinement below upon so poor and watery a diet, he, of course, became exceedingly weak, and could scarcely utter a syllable, and not being anxious to again trust to the brass rod, he obtained through his partner the presence of the steward; whereupon he was requested to bring " the scales;" this being asked in such a feeble voice, coupled with the singularity of the term, that worthy had some difficulty in understanding him, and it was sometime ere the poor gentleman could clearly explain what he required. It turned out to be a ladder, that he might descend without the assistance of his deceitful friend, the brass rod. Having safely landed, and still assisted by the steward, he uttered the words, in a very low and plaintive voice, that "it was von dam nuisance, and he vould not again shail on the vater!" He was in fearful agony, and could not for the world manage to get his legs into his pantaloons without assistance. This at length was accomplished by the steward, and the Frenchman managed to crawl a few yards from his berth.

Among the Cricketers who could not get up at any time during the day, were John Lillywhite, Caffyn, Jackson, and H. H. Stephenson, and they were consequently visited, and the renowned fast bowler wished much for a "back door to Ollerton," his residence in Notts. Caffyn "would not venture to leave England again, under "any circumstances; if he did, he would forfeit £100; and could "not understand however he was induced to ride over such waves, and "see no land. Let me once get back to Reigate, (his residence), and "no more water, in order to play Cricket Matches." John Lillywhite was very ill, but quiet in his berth, not being at all talkative; others were also bad, including Grundy, Lockyer, and Diver, who were seldom seen. Julius Cæsar did not fancy himself so much in the capacity of a sailor as that of a cricketer. Parr, Wisden, Hayward, Carpenter, and Fred. Lillywhite were "as being on shore." The latter was invariably on deck, from midnight till eight bells announced four o'clock, a.m.; when, after partaking of a cup of coffee, either with the first or second mate, he retired to his berth until lunch time. The sea this night was breaking on the deck most fearfully, and for the first time one was reminded, "of a life on the ocean wave." Diver played his part in his usual steady manner, but was not quite "at home," expecting, and, in fact, rather wishing to be "bowled out." Stephenson was "all abroad," but, nevertheless, often paid a visit to "his bunk." Wisden was a thorough sailor, enjoying both meals and his pipe of tobacco; he thought, when at his meals, that "the waves allowed too much for the break," and Parr thought their five ton Leamington roller, and "Charley," with their high priced mare,* might take off the "ridge and ferroll,"

* "Charley" is their Leamington man—the high priced mare cost 50 (s.)

and stop the "bumping."' Singing was attempted this, (Friday), evening, but owing to the condition of the passengers, most of whom were suffering from sickness, the concert was a failure. The chirping cricketers could neither lift up their heads nor their voices, except in the most plaintive strain. The opposite engraving will represent, as nearly as possible, the persons who were sitting in the smoking saloon, on the occasion alluded to, when a storm was raging with all its fury. All the worthy captain's persuasion could not get a ditty, either from Grundy, Caffyn, or Carpenter, who possessed the largest amount of vocal talent among the cricketers.

SATURDAY, September 10th

was a fine morning, and many faces were visible that had not been seen since Thursday. Met this morning, one of the "renowned party," at half past eleven, a.m., who, for some unknown cause, had not been seen at the dinner table since Wednesday. We walked arm and arm by way of mutual support, for the ship was pitching most provokingly. In reply to my question, he said, "he had not been at all poorly the evening before, but only went below for the purpose of arranging the contents of his "chest.'' Ah, you mean "stomach," said I. He then remarked, that he thought I looked white, (my appearance resembling Lockyer's colour in July,) but I expressed my fear that he was going to be ill again; to which he replied, "do you think so?" and immediately retired to his berth, probably to complete the arrangements of the *chest* aforesaid.

We were this morning doing only six and a half knots, and up to this date Parr, Carpenter, Wisden, Cæsar, and Fred. Lillywhite were always seated at the dinner table; others nowhere to be found, only those who still occupied their unenviable seats on deck. Between one and two o'clock the gale abated, and some little time after the wind was more favourable, and the log found us going at nine knots an hour, having done altogether 560 miles. During the day, all, with the exception of Stephenson, seemed pretty well recovered, so much so as to venture upon smoking. The captain, ever ready to serve or entertain us, introduced a game called "shuffle-

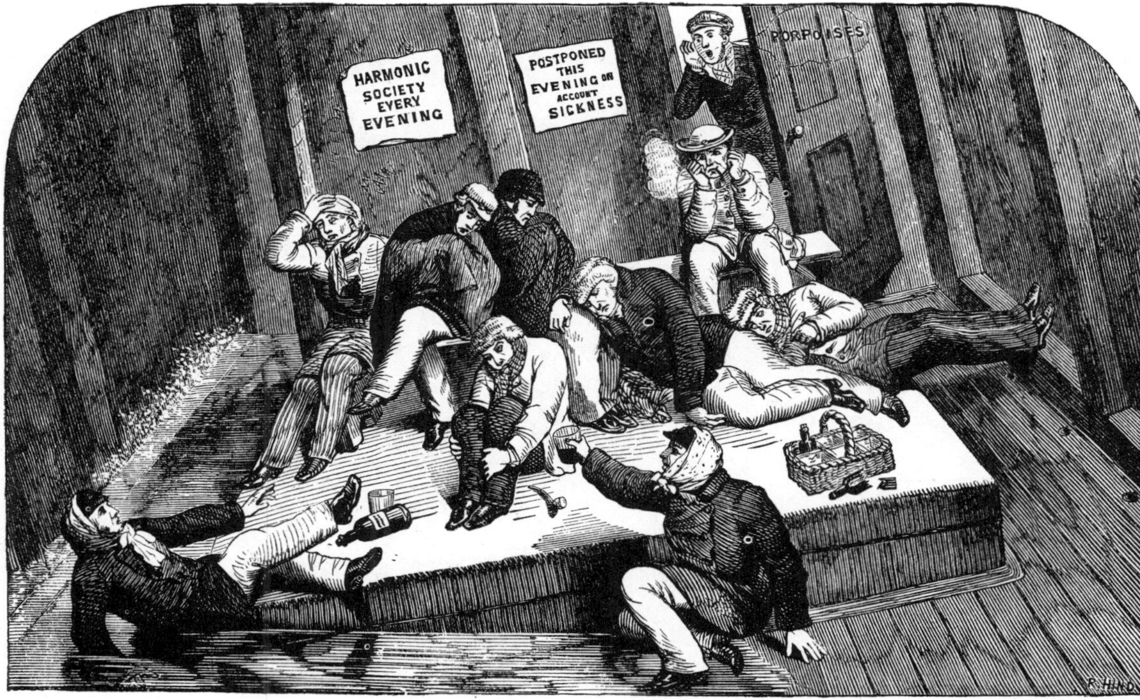

SCENE IN THE SMOKING ROOM.

SHUFFLE BOARD.

board," in which the captain, the engineer, the purser, &c., played with us. The carpenter of the ship chalked the deck, as the opposite engraving will shew.

The game is played thus:—At the distance of eight or nine yards the players slide along the deck a piece of solid wood, about the size of a quoit, and those who get 100 up first wins. Many exciting games were played, to the temporary advantage of the officers of the ship, who, from their experience and knowledge of the "roll of the vessel," had many points in their favor. Matches were made for champagne,—Moet's best, six shillings per bottle. Several games were very exciting, and often caused a large attendance of passengers of both sexes to witness the contests. The purser and engineer were the two best players. This, Saturday afternoon, rain came on, which drove the players to the "smoking" saloon, kindly placed at our disposal by the captain's orders, with his servant boy, "Young Irish Jack," to attend upon us. Whist and loo constituted the amusements of the evening. The "Nova Scotian Harmonic Society" was afterwards effectively established. The smoking saloon was the hatchway, snugly arranged for the purpose; Mr. W. Nicholson, an elderly and a very witty gentleman, from Sheffield, was unanimously voted as president, and which office he filled with the greatest efficiency. The time of meeting was to be half-past seven o'clock each evening, weather and stomachs permitting; a jolly Saturday evening at sea was spent. We drank in the most enthusiastic manner to the health of "wives and sweethearts," and success to the noble ship. A vice-president having been appointed for the meeting on Monday evening, the party retired at eleven o'clock to their respective berths. Distance done during the last twenty-four hours, as per announcement of the log that day, was 160 miles. Much speculation took place each day during luncheon, about "setting the log"; sweeps were got up, and the officers' opinions on the subject were anxiously sought by the "cricketing novices," whose knowledge as to "how the ship was going," was very limited. On

SUNDAY, September 11.

Arrangements had been made for church service, to be performed by the Hon.— Rose, the Solicitor-General of Montreal. A fearful gale however again arose, which precluded the attendance of the passengers. The wind was favourable for Quebec, but it blew a hurricane and rained the whole of the day; when the ship pitched the screw was out of water, and the passengers were scattered about the deck, resembling, as Lockyer thought, very much "a floorer at skittles;" this occurred so frequently during the day, that the "nines" would have been quite common. At half past twelve o'clock the log announced that day 235 miles, notwithstanding the fearful rolling and pitching of the noble ship. During tea an exciting scene occurred. Caffyn in attempting to imbibe the fragrant beverage, had the cup shaken from his hand, and lt was soon smashed below, falling over the banisters, with numerous others, among the berths. The head of an elderly gentleman came into such violent contact with a panel as to split it open, not the panel, but the head, he at the same time good humouredly remarking, that his friends would have some reason for saying that he was a little cracked. A passenger on entering the cabin-door seized hold of the first mate's chair, which was fixed; however, by his weight the chair gave way, and in endeavouring to save himself, he made fast very quickly, owing to a severe roll of the ship, to the captain's chair, placed in a similar position as the chief officer's; this piece of furniture also giving way, the two were dashed against the side of the ship, one being dangerously wounded, and the other very severely bruised. Lurch No. 1 carried away an immense quantity of cups and saucers; No. 2, caused the violent collision between the two gentlemen above alluded to; No. 3, cleared off knives, forks, and spoons; No. 4, plates, dishes, &c.; No. 5, pitched some pickled onions, which Jackson was trying to convey to his mouth into his lap; No. 6, caused a cup of tea, in the waiter's hand, to be deposited in Fred. Lillywhite's lap, having previously destroyed the arrangement of his locks.—[See opposite engraving.]

MONDAY, September 12

was a lovely morning, all quite recovered, and did not want to be "at home;" in fact, they repudiated the idea of being ill, or having been so. A very grand morning for shuffle-board; the matches made were numerous and interesting; Lockyer proved a victim; about 190

SCENE IN THE DINING SALOON.

passengers mustered to witness the contests. Shortly after twelve the rain again coming on, put a stop to the play, and the "talent" retired to the smoking saloon, where whist and loo predominated until the time arrived for the meeting of the Harmonic Society, which was a numerous one. A convivial evening was spent, after a very excellent spread of four courses had been done justice to. The repast was admirably served by the chief steward and his attentive assistants.

Mr. Nicholson, the president, Diver, Grundy, and Carpenter were the principal contributors to harmony. The captain honoured the company with his attendance, and the above vocalists were rapturously applauded, so much so that the question of an extra gallery, and charge for admission was mooted by the managers. At the conclusion of the concert, each evening, the captain's health was drank with such evident enthusiasm, as to leave no doubt as to the soundness of the lungs of those present. A similar compliment the officers of the staff had never before witnessed on the briny ocean nor perhaps ever will again. The log to-day shewed 200 miles, having a head wind. On

TUESDAY, September 13,

the members had sufficiently recovered to call the roll at 9.15. The great Roman commander, Julius Cæsar, ordered all to muster, and discharged them for the day. An important shuffle board match was to be played, and several pounds, as well as bottles of champagne depended upon the result. The contest was between the captain of the ship and Fred. Lillywhite, against Lockyer and John Lillywhite; a most exciting game ensued; the purser was sworn in as marker, and the whole of the passengers, including cabin and steerage, were present. The game proceeded, one heading the other, until the marker announced ninety-nine for White, (Captain and F. L.,) and ninety-five for Black. The latter had the last throw, and of course the odds were in their favour, they having the option of displacing their opponent's pieces, which were on the figures. The White side getting a three, caused their score to be 102, but Lockyer for black removed Fred. Lillywhite's piece from the figure 3, and put his, (Lockyer's), partner's in its place, his own piece of wood going on the "10 on." Here a dispute arose among the contending parties, as to whether white was not entitled to the game, having *first* obtained the required number of 100; Black, however, contended that their "ten on," was obtained by the three he had made by that throw, but, there being no laws, and the circumstance never having happened before, to the recollection of any of the officers, it was agreed that the four should throw again, which resulted in Lockyer and John Lillywhite winning by one only. Shortly after this contest a heavy fog set in, with rain; in this melancholy condition the fog whistle was sounded every two minutes for the whole day and night. All at dinner to-day; concert at night. The log shewed that a distance of 192 miles had been accomplished in twenty-four hours.

WEDNESDAY, September 14.

The fog was much worse, and the whistle still exercising its disagree able office, to the annoyance of the passengers. The wind was still dead against us, with a heavy sea. Saw an enormous number of porpoises; "some tarnation good sport, I guess, there would be with a gun," said a Yankee captain, who was also a "tarnation enquirer," being most inquisitive to know everything about the "doings" of the English party, so that he might invest his dollars.

The doctor having been taken ill, the unfortunate Frenchman had now to go to him for advice. Distance now done was 1,400 miles. All remarkably well, and most of them were at whist during the afternoon. Log to-day 213 miles. A fearful gale again set in, and lasted through the next day.

THURSDAY, September 15.

"Dreadful!" says Caffyn. "Well, plenty of wind about," says Lockyer, but, "not much land," replies John Lillywhite. Hayward, Parr, and others began to enquire of the captain, very seriously, whether it was really dangerous. During this afternoon Parr had unfortunately to encounter a kettle of boiling water in the smoking-saloon, which Cæsar, owing to a roll of the ship, had accidentally upset, he himself measuring his length on the floor of the cabin, among the glasses of grog, &c. This day will long be remembered by all the Cricketers. The gale commenced about seven o'clock in the morning, and the scene, as represented on the opposite page again occurred, and created a hearty laugh among those who were now "hardened down sailors." The waves were mountains high, and one passenger who had crossed the Atlantic sixty times, said he had never experienced it so rough. Again cups and saucers, basins, glasses, knives, spoons, &c., were equally distributed about the saloon, and passengers, were often under the disagreeable necessity of knocking each other down. Two sails were carried away to-day, and it was expected that a number of sailors engaged aloft would also follow. At 11.30, p.m. when all the passengers had retired, the engines were found to be damaged, and they were of course stopped; this fact, whether in our berths or out, would soon become known and felt by all; we accordingly made no progress whatever, having a head wind. It was not long before a great many passengers were anxiously making enquiries as to the amount of injury, but no one could get further information than, "Oh! merely to try whether she will answer to her sails;" the trial, however, lasted three hours. Up to twelve o'clock this day we had done, during the twenty-four hours, 250 miles, altogether 1,650. We had no concert this evening, being totally unable either to sit, stand, walk, or do anything but to bring one's self to an anchor on deck, and stand the drenching. Some managed by dint of perseverance to remain in the smoking saloon, but the agonising expression of their faces would have been a fortune to Leech. At bed time numerous accidents occurred among the passengers; one young gentleman especially had the misfortune to break the bridge of his nose, by falling from the top to the bottom of the cabin stairs. The Captain was busily engaged among his men, giving strict orders.

FRIDAY MORNING, September 16.

There was no improvement in the weather, and nearly the whole of us remained in our berths, for we were so very frequently disturbed in our rest, during the whole of the night, that we were scarcely disposed to turn out during the day. Towards evening the gale abated; we had only been doing three knots an hour. We saw during the day an immense quantity of porpoises, which, by their apparently unwieldy gambols, caused great amusement. At twelve the log shewed, from the last return, that we had only progressed eighty miles, making altogether, 1730; the afternoon was very cold, and was spent at whist. We now began to entertain the expectation of shortly sighting land. Concert in the evening, and all as jolly as sand-boys. Our worthy, respected, and talented president of the *Nova Scotian* Harmonic Society was in high glee on the occasion of our meeting, and having explained the cause of his absence, which appeared to be totally unavoidable, he immediately took his seat, and harmony was the prevailing feature, " the Jew in the Corner " was the favourite. About eleven o'clock, p.m., that night, some two or three who remained on deck, had the pleasure, for the first time in their lives, of seeing some icebergs. Notwithstanding that these stupendous fabrics were beautiful objects for contemplation by day, they were particularly awkward customers to come in contact with at night. Though the chief officer himself stood at the bow, with his quick eye watching a-head, twice we came too close to them to be at all pleasant. The northern lights were splendid. On

SATURDAY, September 17,

many of the passengers were awoke early in the morning, by the novel and startling cry of " icebergs a-head! icebergs on the larboard bow!" and, " icebergs on the beam!" and all ran hastily to the deck, and there discovered that they were in the midst of large numbers of them. We had an opportunity of forming an estimate of their size, for a large ship was sailing past one of the latter, and her main-top-gallant-mast only reached one-third the height of the berg. In calculating its total altitude, we did not forget to take into consideration the fact of there being at least eight feet of ice below water, for every foot above; some navigators go so far as to say there are eleven. [See opposite engraving.]

Concert this evening, which lasted until eleven o'clock, when, all but the sleepless ones retired, more particularly as land was expected to be seen in the early hours of the morn of

MEETING AN ICEBERG.

SUNDAY, September 18th.

We were in a fog, but it having at length cleared away, the welcome cry of " land, ho!" sent a thrill to all hearts. We borrowed the chief officer's glass, and saw in the distance the bleak, bluff, inhospitable-looking coast of Newfoundland, with its cliffs, and snow-covered mountains; this was our first glimpse of land for ten days, and we gazed upon it with rapture. Soon after we doubled Cape Race, and, by and by, the revolving light upon Cape Ray became visible. By seven o'clock in the morning we were off a lovely little island, and could see the green trees waving upon the heights. In another six or seven hours the captain ascertained that he had taken a wrong course, (owing to the fog and the compasses) going up the "White bay," instead of the Gulf of St. Lawrence. By this we lost fourteen hours, about 140 miles. It was, however, a lovely trip, water like a pond; there were rugged rocks on each side of us, water-falls, and a quantity of bears and wolves. We had arrived within about two miles of the end of the bay, before our error was discovered, we then made a turn round, and enjoyed very much the Sunday afternoon's excursion. All the passengers were in strong force this afternoon, both ladies and gentlemen, and the dinner-table had its full complement—the Cricketers especially doing ample justice to the contents of the table, knowing that all rough usage on the part of the sea was at an end, and that having once got the right course, and sighted Belle Isle, we should have 700 miles of river and splendid views, among which were conspicuous the White huts of the French settlers.

MONDAY, September 19.

At three o'clock this morning we sighted the light-house of Belle Isle, and on we steamed at eleven knots an hour. At 6.30 we saluted the worthies who officiate in that lovely department. Plenty of icebergs. Passed the North Britain, bound for Liverpool, at five, p.m., another of the company's steamers, distance from us about 100 yards. Three hearty cheers were given from both ships as we passed, and on the side of the North Britain was written in chalk, " Persia not arrived." This steamer left Liverpool on September 3rd, four days before us, so that she encountered a severe voyage. Early in the evening the Captain remarked, " they are making pretty merry there in the smoking saloon, " Whose voice is that, Tom ?" " The Jew in the corner," replied Lockyer; they have again voted him to the chair. Then Carpenter struck up with—

> " There's a sweet little cherub that sits up aloft,
> To keep watch for the life of poor Jack."

which ditty was speedily followed by Grundy's performance of his celebrated " Dolly Dobbs," by which time Captain Borland, and the engineer, were among the company, as well as several aristocratic passengers, who were anxious to spend some time with the English party, ere they separated at Quebec. The chorus of Grundy's song, was as follows, and is his own composition.

> " Wigel wagel, shigel shagel,
> Rigel ragel dom ;
> Rumpty doodle, tadel fudel,
> Didel, dadel dom."

A specimen of rhyming seldom met with on board a ship, and which here, as elsewhere, received an unusual amount of approbation. This evening was a very merry one, and the song, jest, and merry glee were kept going till past twelve o'clock.

TUESDAY, September 20.

Passed Anticosti island, which is half the size of England. The day was spent at shuffle-board and whist. The huts of the settlers were now far more numerous. Very dull day. Some Americans were talking of their revolvers to-day, and " guessed " at many things.

WEDNESDAY, September 21.

The pilot landed at Father point, 11.20, a.m., we were then about 150 miles from Quebec. Fishing smacks of all descriptions were continually passing. Of the scenery up the river to Quebec, one cannot well have the assurance to attempt a description ; pen cannot describe it ; the brush cannot paint it ; the poet and the artist must throw both

ST. LAWRENCE HOTEL.

away in despair; we never beheld anything so beautiful. The pure sky above us, the magnificent St. Lawrence beneath and beyond, the loveliness of the shores, strewn with many a picturesque village, and exquisite little church; together with the bold, dark outline of the stately mountains on either side of us, formed a glorious picture that could be gazed on at once with wonder and delight.

Shortly before one o'clock on the morning of—

THURSDAY, September 22,

we heard a hoarse, sullen, rumbling sound, like the roar of distant artillery, which broke the stillness of the morning; the heavy anchor had plunged into the blue depths beneath us, and the voyage was ended. We remained on board until half past five o'clock. Three hundred feet above us, perched upon a dizzy precipice, frowned the city of Quebec. The sentry, with his bright bayonet flashing, was gazing over the ramparts, and looked like a red insect shouldering a rather large silver toothpick. We had no leisure for further observation, as in another moment the *Nova Scotian* was fast to the wharf, and we soon leaped on shore, when everything appeared as if it were on the roll. Without the slightest inconvenience at the Customs, the authorities of which were extremely polite and courteous, we at once had the whole of our baggage transferred to the railway station, only a few yards off, where we met Mr. Baker, a gentlemen to whose kindness and attention the cricketers owe a large debt of gratitude. We shortly afterwards, per special train, made our way to Montreal, a distance of 179 miles.

During the time our "special" was getting steam up, &c. it came on to rain, but not as it rains in England, for the drops were the size of quarter-dollar pieces, and half a dozen of them were sufficient to ensure a thorough wetting. With the exception of a desk, containing 120 sovereigns, everybody and everything arrived safely at the St. Lawrence Hall, Montreal, followed by the desk the next morning. The Eleven were exceedingly well received by those assembled. On the opposite page is an engraving of the hotel, which is double as large as any hotel in Canada, and it is scarcely necessary to say, is the first in Canada; so much so, that it is the residence of the Governor-General, when he is at Montreal. The proprietors were large subscribers to the match here, as they are to all manly games and exercises for which Old England is distinguished; they possess "crack" horses, dogs, &c., and are never backward in their efforts to promote sport of every description.

The treatment at the hotel is of the most liberal description. The visitors are awoke in the morning by the sounding of an immense gong, the sonorous tones of which penetrate to the remotest sleeping apartments. Upon descending to the breakfast room, between 200 and 300 guests were found seated, and engaged upon breaking their fast. Luncheon is laid at twelve o'clock, and consists of cold meats, poultry, vegetables, pickles, &c., which remain upon table about two hours. At four o'clock, the gong is again sounded for dinner, which generally comprises an abundant supply of soups, fish, poultry, joints, pies, Indian corn, *&c.*, at which the whole of the visitors again assemble, very few preferring to dine separately, or in their own rooms. Tea immediately follows; and from nine till eleven o'clock, supper may be had. This, with a spacious sleeping apartment, of which the visitor has a key, together with an excellent bed, and ready and obliging attendants, is covered by an outlay of about two and-a-half dollars per diem.

FRIDAY, September 23,

was a wet day, or play would have begun, although the Eleven would not have been "up to the mark" after so recent a landing. Visited the much talked of Victoria bridge. We now proceed to the play:—

ELEVEN OF ENGLAND *v.* TWENTY-TWO OF LOWER CANADA.

SATURDAY, September 24.

Many days had been lost by thousands of anxious spectators, who had been in Montreal ever since Monday, waiting the coming of the Eleven, who, owing to the rough voyage they had encountered, and other unforeseen circumstances, did not arrive at the time expected (September 17 or 18). It would be impossible to describe the excitement that prevailed in the city on the above day morning, when it became known that the contest would be commenced. During the previous day the English party visited the ground, and F. Lillywhite's printing tent, which he had taken from England, was also erected and ready for work. Reporters were present from all parts of the States, who were very active and pressing in their demand for information, and most especially for the first use of the telegraph wires. But little betting took place. Among the Americans much "talk" ensued about the New York match. This was all—for we did not see them part with any dollars, nor did they speculate upon the event. The weather was not very fine, but cleared up towards the middle of the day.

At about eleven o'clock, the British Eleven were on the ground, and the natives seemed very much amused at seeing them at practice. The company soon became very large, and by the time "play" was called there were not less than 3,000 spectators. The large stand on the right hand side of the gateway was soon filled with ladies; on the left there were a great many carriages. On the lower part of the ground a tent was erected to supply refreshments to the public, close to which was a smaller one for the English only. Soon after twelve o'clock the Eleven were seen in the field. Every man knew his place. Jackson and Caffyn started bowling, Lockyer at the wicket, Parr point, Diver long-stop, Stephenson middle-wicket, Cæsar cover-point, Lillywhite long-leg, Grundy short-leg. G. Swain, Esq. and Lieutenant Surman took the bat first. and played very steadily, but could not make many runs, the ground being very dead, The bowling of the Eleven was anything but good; the sea voyage seemed to have taken effect on all the bowlers. No stand was made until Mr. Pickering went in. He played very well, and reminded the Englishmen of what he was when he played at Lord's. His forward play and cutting were the same as in former days. He, with Mr. Daley, displayed some first-class cricket. Mr. Daley is a young player, with good defence, and can hit well all round. His 19 was the largest score. He made two splendid cuts for three each, one good drive for three, and two twos at the leg. These two gentlemen caused a change in the bowling; Stephenson was put on at Caffyn's end, but he, like the others, was not up to the mark; nor Wisden, who was tried at Jackson's end. At last Parr went on at Stephenson's end, and it was soon found that the Canadians were not up to the slows, for Parr made sad work with them. No other double figure was made than that of Mr. Daley. At half-past four the Twenty-two were all out, with a score of 84 runs—by no means a bad one, considering the state of the ground.

After the usual time allowed between the innings, the Eleven sent Wisden and Grundy, to the bowling of Harding and Fisher. It was a very bad light; the sun was going down behind the mountains, and that caused a particular glare, which the "John Bulls," as the Canadians called them, were not used to; and it was well there was so little time to play, or they would probably have lost two or three wickets. Hardy bowled Grundy off his legs in his second over. Hayward went next, and, with Wisden, stayed until time was called. This ended the first day's play.

On Sunday, the Eleven were taken round the mountain by some of the Members of the Montreal club. They saw a sight which they will never forget. At this time of year the maple trees change their colour, and present a beautiful appearance.

Monday morning came in with fine cricketing weather. The quiet Sunday seemed to have done the Eleven good; every man was practising early. The ground was soon filled, the stand being quite a spectacle. About half-past eleven o'clock Wisden and Hayward took their places at the wickets. Wisden put three more runs to his former score, when he gave a chance in the slip, which was taken. Caffyn joined Hayward, and both began playing in earnest. The ground was much better than on Saturday. Hayward made some splendid hits—one to the leg out of the ground, which very much pleased the company, and brought forth great applause. Caffyn made some splendid cuts, in his usual style, which were much admired. All seemed to know good play from bad. These two were playing well, when Hayward contrived to run out. His score was a well-got 17. George Parr now made his appearance. The bowling was rather loose, and the splendid batting of Caffyn was much appreciated. The bowling was what is termed in England completely "collared." Before either were out 50 runs were got. Caffyn's timber was lowered by Mr. Fisher. His 18 were got by some fine hits, cuts, and leg-hits principally. Julius Cæsar was the next to take the bat; but, unfortunately, he played the ball against his foot, and it rolled to the wicket with sufficient force to cause the bail to fall off. Diver followed, but it was some time before he could score. He and Parr played steadily together until Parr received a trimmer from Mr. Fisher, which caused him to retire. He was not got rid of until he put 24 runs to his name. His leg hitting was good. Six wickets were now down for 74 runs. No stand was made until Lockyer and Jackson got together. The former, in his usual style, got 19, and not out; and Jackson 10. About half-past three the Eleven were all out, with a score of 117, being 32 ahead in the first innings. After a short time the Twenty-two went to the wickets again; but the bowling of Jackson and Parr was too good to allow many runs to be made. The fielding of the Eleven was particularly good, and Lockyer's wicket-keeping surprised the Canadians. So much pleased were they that they made Lockyer a handsome present of money, we heard not less than £20. The fielding was so good that half the Twenty-two were afraid to move off their ground, The whole of them were got out for 63 runs, leaving the Eleven 32 to get to win. Lockyer and Hayward went in first, and scored 14, when Hayward struck a ball upwards, which was beautifully caught at point. Caffyn joined Lockyer, and those two ran the score up till it was a tie, when Lockyer was bowled off his leg. Diver went in, and the first over got the winning run. Thus the first match resulted in favour of England in Canada.

The Canadians, throughout the match, evinced no small amount of cricketing ability, and had they been playing against an Eleven less skilled in the game than their opponents, the score would no doubt, have presented a very different total; but the team that had been selected to sustain the reputation of Old England, in this, her national sport, comprised the best professional cricketers of the day, who spared no efforts to ensure victory for their first match on a foreign soil. They, by no means, held the play of the Canadians too lightly, but carefully and steadily watched every opportunity of adding to their score, and of preventing their opponents from going ahead. On the first day, as before remarked, they had scarcely got rid of the effects of their sea voyage, and, therefore, their bowling lacked the steadiness and precision which prevailed in subsequent matches.

On the following page is the correct score from the type, as printed on the ground, by Fred. Lillywhite, at Montreal.

CORRECT SCORE

FROM F. LILLYWHITE'S PRINTING TENT OF LORD'S & KENNINGTON OVAL LONDON.

At Montreal, Lower Canada, 11 of England *v*. 22 of Lower Canada.
Saturday, Monday, and Tuesday, September 24, 26, & 27.

Twenty Two. First Innings.		Second Innings.	
G. Swain, Esq., b Caffyn	4	c Jackson b Caffyn	1
Lieut. Surman, R.C.R., c Caffyn b Jackson	4	l b w b Caffyn	7
Lieut. Symons, R.A., c Jackson, b Caffyn	2	run out	1
Lieut. Bonner, R.A., b Jackson	0	st Lockyer b Jackson	6
F. Fisher, Esq., l b w b Jackson	0	run out	3
F. Fourdrinier, Esq., c Grundy b Jackson	6	b Jackson	5
S. Hardinge, Esq., b Caffyn	0	c Lillywhite b Parr	0
— Ravenhill, Esq., c Jackson b Caffyn	2	b Jackson	0
Capt. Earle, run out	4	c Lillywhite b Jackson	6
W. P. Pickering, Esq., b Caffyn	8	c Lockyer b Jackson	0
Capt. King, b Jackson	8	c Stephenson b Jackson	3
J. G. Daley, Esq., b Parr	10	run out	0
Webber Smith, Esq., b Jackson	3	hit wicket b Parr	2
G. Bacon, Esq., run out	4	b Parr	2
S. Morgan. Esq., c Wisden b H. H. Stephenson	0	l b w b Parr	0
W. Swettenham, b Parr	3	c Lockyer b Parr	1
J. Smith, Esq., c Stephenson, b Parr	6	b Parr	17
W. Napier, Esq.. st Lockyer b Parr	0	c Grundy b Parr	0
W. Ellis, Esq., c and b Parr	2	b Parr	0
R. S. Pryor, Esq , b Jackson	3	c Caffyn b Parr	1
C. H. Tilstone, Esq., c Lockyer b Parr	0	not out	0
J. M. Kerr, Esq., not out	1	c Cæsar b Parr	2
Byes 4, leg byes 2	6	Leg byes 4, wide 2	6
Total	85	Total	63

The English Eleven.	First Innings.	Second Innings.	
J. Grundy b Hardinge	2		
J. Wisden c Hardinge b Fisher	7		
T. Hayward, run out	17	c Bonner b Smith	10
W. Caffyn b Fisher	18	not out	4
G. Parr b Fisher	24		
J. Cæsar b Fisher	0		
A. Diver c Pickering b Napier	3	not out	1
John Lillywhite, b Napier	4		
T. Loekyer, not out	19	b J. Smith	10
H. H. Stephenson, b Fisher	2		
J. Jackson, b J. Smith	10		
Byes 5, wides 6	11	Byes 2, wides 5	7
Total	117	Total	32

ANALYSIS OF THE BOWLING.

CANADA—FIRST INNINGS.

	Balls.	*Runs.*	*M'n Overs.*	*Wickets.*	*Wides.*	*No Balls.*
J. Jackson	184	21	31	7	0	0
Caffyn	112	33	12	5	0	0
H.H.Stephenson	68	10	10	1	0	0
Wisden	40	7	6	0	0	0
G. Parr	44	8	5	6	0	0

CANADA—SECOND INNINGS.

Jackson	100	20	14	6	1	0
Caffyn	32	12	3	2	1	0
Parr	81	19	9	10	0	0
Wisden	24	6	2	0	0	0

ENGLAND—FIRST INNINGS.

Hardinge	68	24	7	1	2	0
Fisher	128	53	11	5	1	0
Napier	76	24	5	2	3	0
J. U. Smith	13	5	0	1	9	0

ENGLAND—SECORD INNINGS.

J. U. Smith	28	10	3	2	4	0
Fisher	8	7	0	0	1	0
Hardinge	20	8	1	0	0	0

During the above match two Yankees were heard talking about the play; one asked the other what he thought of the Eleven. "Oh, they are smart chaps," he replied; "but I reckon they will find their match at New York." The New York players appeared very confident of beating theEleven, for they were talking about betting 2 and 3 to 1 on themselves. The batting of the Montreal Clubwas much better than might have been expected. They play fast bowling well, but we should advise them to practise against the slows a little more, or they will be sure to lose the greater part of their matches; the fielding was not good, owing, perhaps, to the rough state of the ground, as they seemed to get to the ball well, but could not pick it up clean. Some of the bowling was very good, but we should strongly recommend them first to try to bowl straight, and then put on the pace. Their chief endeavour seems to be to bowl as fast as they can—the very last thing that ought to be done, particularly on a dead ground. The bowling of the Eleven was not up to the mark at any part of the game; neither Jackson nor Caffyn being on the wicket. The fielding, however, with Lockyer's wicket-keeping, excited the admiration of all spectators, and it is needless to say that the Eleven were delighted at the result.

SUPPLEMENTARY MATCH.

After the great event was over, another match was commenced, with six of the All England Eleven against Six of the United All England Eleven, with five Canadians on each side. The match was played for the benefit of the English players, and was commenced, although only two overs were bowled when the wet put a stop to the play for that day. Wednesday being also very wet, it was impossible for any play to take place. Thursday was fine. The United won the toss, and sent Caffyn and Grundy to the wickets, against the bowling of Parr and Jackson. There was some good cricket shown. Wisden played a good innings, as did also Lillywhite and Carpenter. The Canadians were so pleased with the specimens of cricket they had seen, that they pressed the Eleven to stop another day and go on with the match, which they agreed to do. Some very good play was exhibited on both sides. The United won the match in one innings. Score:—

UNITED.

Caffyn, b Jackson	13
Grundy, l b w b Parr	0
Carpenter, b Hayward	32
Webber Smith, Esq., b Jackson	0
Lockyer, l b w b Hayward	8
Pickering, Esq., b Jackson	0
John Lillywhite, b Jackson	53
Wisden, c Parr, b Stephenson	43
Fisher, Esq., not out	14
Morgan, Esq., b Stephenson	2
Bacon, Esq., b Parr	7
Byes 9, leg-byes 3, wides 4	16
Total	188

ALL ENGLAND.

First Innings.		Second Innings.	
Daley, Esq., c Grundy b Caffyn	0	b Wisden	0
Cæsar, c Carpenter b Caffyn	14	b Caffyn	11
Hayward, c Carpenter b Grundy	18	c Carpenter b Wisden	0
Hardinge, Esq., c Carpenter b Caffyn	0	not out	0
Diver, c Carpenter b Wisden	14	b Wisden	1
Swettenham, Esq., c Carpenter b Caffyn	3	b Wisden	0
Parr, c Lockyer b Caffyn	0	c Smith b Caffyn	24
J. U. Smith, Esq., b Wisden	6	b Caffyn	1
F. Fourdrinier, st Lockyer b Carpenter	19	c Wisden b Carpenter	4
Jackson. l b w b Carpenter	9	run out	9
H. H. Stephenson, not out	6	c Carpenter b Wisden	2
Leg-bye	1	Leg-bye	1
Total	90	Total	44

DINNER TO THE ENGLISH PARTY.

This dinner took place in the St. Lawrence Hotel on Saturday, September 24. About one hundred sat down to table.

F. G. Johnson, Esq., presided, and A. Heward, Esq., filled the vice-chair.

The band of the 17th Regiment was present, and during the whole evening played a number of appropriate airs.

After cricketer's justice had been done to the dinner, the cloth was removed, and

The Chairman proposed "The Queen." He said that Englishmen never gave a preface for the Queen. He should therefore simply give "The Queen."

Drunk with loud cheers, band playing "God save the Queen." The Vice-president sung "God save the Queen," the whole company joining.

The next toast was "His Royal Highness the Prince Consort and the Royal Family." The Chairman said he should not make a speech to introduce that toast to cricketers, but, like the previous one, simply give it.

Toast drunk with all the honours. Band.

The Chairman next proposed "The Governor-General." He said as the hearts of all of them were filled with loyalty, they would drink the toast with enthusiasm.

Toast drunk amid loud and continued cheering, and all the honours.

The Chairman next gave "The Army and Navy." He said, when the toasts which Englishmen drink first on these occasions were disposed of, they are succeeded by one that is always received with great enthusiasm. The previous ones have required no comment from me, and I am sure that this one will not either. It is not for me to extol their achievements, they are known to all wherever civilization prevails.

Drunk with all the honours.

The Chairman next gave the toast of "Our Guests." He said, in giving the toast of the Queen, I promised you to be as brief as possible. I have, I think I may venture to say, adhered to that promise. But an occasion now presents itself when it will be very difficult indeed to carry out that promise. I do not propose to make you a long speech—nothing could be less acceptable than such a speech, and yet it is very difficult to resist the gratification of attempting to express the pleasure I really feel—which all here feel—in having the "Elevens" of Old England—(cheers)—the "Elevens" of England, I say, dining with us in Montreal for the first time, and not only with us for the first time, but the first time they have ever dined together on this continent.

(Loud cheers.) And none, I trust, will forget to whom we owe this pleasure—to whose exertions are mainly due this great event in our Montreal existence. It is not necessary to name to you the name of the captain of your cricket club here in Montreal; it is not necessary to name the name of Pickering—(loud cheers)—nor that you should be made aware that he it is who has the honour of having originated this project, and of having carried it out with a degree of ability in detail only equalled by the original thought itself. Now, gentlemen, this is not vain and inflated language. I have lived in Montreal for twenty-two years, and I may say that, apart from some very small attempts at playing on St. Helen's Island, I was a member of the very first cricket club ever got up in Montreal. And I know that if even five or six years ago we had talked of getting out the Eleven of All England to play a match on Canadian ground, we should have been laughed to scorn. Therefore, there is due to Mr. Pickering a very great deal of credit for having originated the project and so successfully carried it through to its fulfilment. (Hear, hear.) I will not attempt to draw a picture of the merits of cricketing, because that is a very trite theme—one that may be seen in any newspaper—one on which all have written and spoken, who have written or spoken at all on the subject of cricketing. You all know what Englishmen are capable of, what they have done, and what they can do. And this, I say, is attributable in no slight measure to the cricket field and the hunting ground, the rivers whereon the youth of England row, the fields wherein they play cricket, and the glorious country through which they ride. Boys are taught upon the playground to be gentlemen in the highest acceptation of the word; they are not taught to be gentlemen in the sense of a class as distinguished from other classes, but in the highest sense of the word—that is to say, in the sense of superiority in morals and in conduct, and in carrying out that great rule in life, "to do to others as you would be done by." (Cheers.) This teaching, which makes cricketers, the sons of plain artisans, entitled to sit with us, and according to which teaching they are received by us with the right hand of fellowship as our equals—that teaching, I say, is no unimportant part of the education of a gentleman. I have said that I would not attempt to extol the manly game of cricket, but there are some thoughts which strike me in connection with it. We live in a country, one of the most glorious dependencies of the British Crown, in which are numerous varieties of races, of creeds, of opinions, of matters political, commercial, and otherwise. May not a lesson be learned from the game in which you have this day been engaged—a lesson of moderation, a lesson of good sense? May we not be taught that there may be differences without animosity, emulation without enmity—that people may rival each other not only in cricket, but in all other pursuits of life, and be like brothers, and remain so. I hope that the Eleven of England, when they go home, may be able to give a good account of the country; that, with the exception of the weather, which has been so disagreeable since their arrival, and has prevented them from travelling as much as they desired, they may be able to express themselves pleased with their reception here. And I hope they will take home with them the desire which I feel, and express on your behalf and my own, that they may consider themselves not strangers to us, but as if they were our own brothers, and of the same flesh and blood, as in reality they are. But I hope that there is one thing that they will not be able to say when they go home. They have amongst them a martial gentleman, one who could speak in a martial manner—Julius Cæsar. And I hope that, unlike the Roman chief, he will not have it to say, on his return to his own country, "*Veni, vidi, vici.*" (Loud cheers.)

Toast drunk with all honours and loud cheering, which continued for some time.

Mr. Carpenter sang "When first I went to sea."

Mr. George Parr rose and briefly replied.

The Chairman then called upon Wisden for a toast, who rose and briefly made allusion to the spirit exhibited by the Lower Canadians in inviting them out to this country. He merely proposed the health of Mr. Pickering.

The toast was drank with Highland honours, and loud and continued cheering.

Mr. Pickering responded. He said he must thank them heartily for the manner in which they had drank his health. The person who deserved all the credit for bringing about the match was one well known to all present, but to many he was a man in every sense of the word—

a Christian of the most philanthropic views. He alluded to Mr. Wilder. Without taking up any further time, he would return thanks for the honour they had done him. If the Montreal Cricket Club had done anything, it was owing to the aid they had received from the citizens of Montreal, who came forward with great spirit when they were appealed to, and lent, with great liberality, a helping hand. He concluded by proposing the health of the Chairman. (Loud cheers.)

Mr. Johnson, in reply, stated that the toast was so unexpected that he could scarcely respond to it. They could not expect, however, that he would enlarge upon such a theme as himself. In his youth he had been a cricketer, and had ever cherished a love for the noble game; but now, owing to his professional avocations, he could not indulge in it. He would tell them something that perhaps they had not heard of. Some time since he had the honour of being the Governor of the Red River Settlement—a settlement founded by the energy of Englishmen, and the capital of the Hudson's Bay Company. Perhaps they would be astonished to hear him state that even in that distant settlement they had a cricket club. He recollected that on the starting of the club there they had no bat or ball. However, with the assistance of a carpenter and shoemaker, these were soon manufactured, and many capital games ensued. Every fine afternoon it used to be customary to play. He had this day received intelligence from Red River, to the effect that the game was still kept up with the usual spirit. He would not be surprised if, in ten years hence, the All England Eleven played a game with the inhabitants of Red River. (Loud and continued cheers.) He had been ridiculed once at that place, because he said that next year a steamboat would arrive there. Strange to say, his words were fulfilled. He concluded by wishing them many a happy game of cricket.

Mr. Wisden proposed the health of Mr. Daly. (Cheers, and drunk with cheers.)

Mr. Daly replied in a very happy manner, thanking the gentleman who had proposed his health for the very flattering encomiums he had passed upon his playing that day. He esteemed it an honour to play with the English Eleven, and he looked upon the match between the clubs as an object not to be obliterated from his memory. He had tried to do his best, and had not expected to play in such circumstances. He could say that the Montrealers had done far better than they expected to do before the match commenced. (Cheers.)

Other toasts were proposed, and the conviviality was kept until twelve o'clock, when the company dispersed.

SATURDAY, October 1st.

Up to Friday evening, September 30th, we made the Montreal cricket ground our rendezvous, and on the next morning at six o'clock started for

NEW YORK,

under the careful guidance of Messrs. Pickering and Baker, who had made all necessary arrangements with the Railway Company, for the purpose of securing our arrival safe in that city, but which was not accomplished until after frequent changing and shifting from cars of one Company to those of another, causing considerable inconvenience, as the baggage had also to be removed, which was not effected in the *most careful manner*, especially the box on wheels, containing Lillywhite's Printing Tent, which apparatus was as often on the top end as on its wheels. Thus, after a most tiresome journey, (not rendered more endurable by the incivility of the company's porters), we reached Albany, where the "New World" river-boat was awaiting our arrival. Every civility was, however, shown us, upon reaching the territories of the United States, by the custom-house officers, in consequence of the baggage being marked "Cricketers of England." The distance from the station at Albany to the river is upwards of a mile, and the road being very bad, we experienced considerable difficulty in conveying our baggage, which, however, was eventually carried to the boat-side, and safely put on board. The portmanteaus and hatboxes gave unmistakeable proof of the severe bruises they had encountered during the one mile of conveyance. It was the greatest wonder in the world that Lilly's box was not smashed all to pieces, a fate which would certainly have happened to it, had it not been for his own interference and bustling. The luggage was thrown about in the most reckless and shameful manner, and we are only surprised that the authorities allow

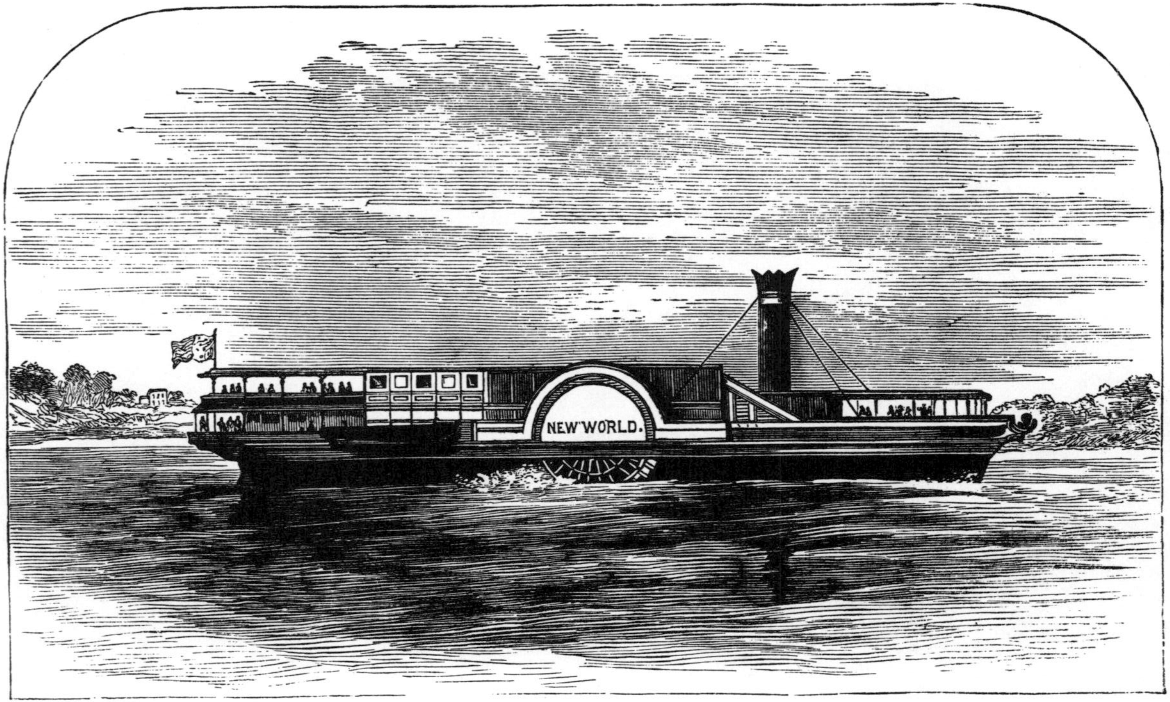

THE RIVER BOAT, "NEW WORLD."

such abominable treatment. To all our requests for gentler usage, we received insulting replies, and less regard for our property; and we were even threatened that it should be left behind. Having at last boarded the "New World," and having secured our bedroom key for one dollar each, we at length found ourselves below, where were numerous black waiters, serving up what they termed "chops!" There were upwards of four hundred passengers on board, sitting in all postures. We made a start on the Saturday evening, at eight o'clock, and, after a night's travelling on the river, we arrived at New York at seven o'clock, on Sunday morning—the river-boat representing something similar to the opposite sketch.

It was ten o'clock ere we arrived at the Astor House, a distance of 450 miles from Montreal. No arrangements were made for our arrival—probably from the want of information as to the time and manner of our arrival. The day was a lovely one, and during the afternoon we visited the Hoboken ground. The hotel was full, and great excitement prevailed the whole of the day. Upwards of two thousand persons were on the ground on Sunday afternoon!

MONDAY, October 18th.

ELEVEN OF ENGLAND *v.* TWENTY-TWO OF THE UNITED STATES.

The above match, under the able management of the St. George's Cricket Club, was began this morning, the weather being all that a cricketer could desire. At 10 o'clock, a.m., an "immense stir" was observable at the Astor House, where thousands had assembled, in order to have a peep at the "English champions." Shortly afterwards we were informed by the president of the club—Mr. Waller—that all was in readiness to be conveyed to the ground. Accordingly, the Cricketers made their appearance on the steps of the hotel, and immediately they were most enthusiastically received, and loudly cheered, by the multitude, as they wended their way down the steps towards the "four-in-hand" prepared for their reception; the horses were beautifully decorated with the American and English flags, as well as a multiplicity of flowers. We crossed the ferry without alighting, and soon found ourselves on the ground at Hoboken, where, at that early hour, were upwards of five thousand spectators. The preparations for the convenience of the public were on the grandest scale imaginable, and evidently had involved an immense outlay. The ground had only been newly laid in the spring, and was therefore not in such good order as is requisite to play the game as it should be played. The English party received every courtesy, and were immediately conducted to a marquee erected for them, where, after the wickets had been decidedly arranged upon, the toss for the choice of innings was effected. England won, but in consequence of the deadness of the ground, and the almost certainty of improvement, they decided to put their opponents in first. We cannot enlarge upon the play, as we saw but little worthy of notice. Scarcely any tolerable batting on the part of the Twenty-two was exhibited, which appeared to, and probably did, arise more from nervousness than any other cause. England, too, showed but little cricket, owing to the somewhat reckless style of the American bowling, though their "hitting," in some cases, was brilliant, especially that of Hayward and Carpenter. John Lillywhite was unable to play, in consequence of a bad hand, which he had greatly injured while obtaining his long score at Montreal; and he therefore officiated as umpire.

It appeared to us that it was pretty evident that the gathering of about 25,000 spectators on the ground, was not caused by any public desire for triumph on either side, but that those who attended each day seemed to be simply actuated by curiosity as to the manner of playing the game of cricket, with a natural desire to see the men who had accomplished so long a journey, and become so famous as players in England. Thus far, they effected their purpose; the ground, and the want of more talent opposed to them, however, prevented the Eleven from exhibiting that masterly display which they have so frequently shown in all parts of England. We may also add that, owing to the excellent arrangements made by the managing committee, the most perfect order prevailed, so that the spectators experienced none of the regrets that are too common at meetings of large assemblies. Should the States be fortunate enough to secure a first-class bowler, there will be no difficulty in bringing forward cricketers; but until then, we can offer them little hope on that score. The weather throughout was beautiful, and it was, consequently, agreed that another match should be commenced on the Thursday, for the benefit of the English players. We now append the correct score.

CORRECT SCORE

FROM F. LILLYWHITE'S PRINTING TENT

OF LORD'S & KENNINGTON OVAL LONDON.

At Hoboken, New York, Eleven of England *v.* 22 of the United States.

Monday, Tuesday, and Wednesday, October 3rd, 4th, and 5th, 1859.

Twenty-two.	First Innings.		Second Innings.	
— Long	b Parr	6	c Carpenter b Wisden	7
R. Waller	run out	0	st Lockyer b Caffyn	0
H Sharp	st Lockyer b Jackson	1	c & b Caffyn	5
W. Hammond	c Hayward b Parr	6	b Caffyn	0
A. H. Gibbes	b Jackson	0	c Lockyer b Caffyn	0
J. W. S. Scarlett	l b w b Parr	4	c Carpenter b Caffyn	1
A. Marsh	l b w b Jackson	0	c Wisden b Caffyn	0
W. Wilby	b Parr	3	b Caffyn	0
T. Senior	hit w b Parr	3	c Carpenter b Caffyn	1
H. Wright	c Lockyer b Parr	1	b Caffyn	5
J. Higham	b Jackson	1	b Caffyn	0
— Head	b Jackson	0	c Lockyer b Caffyn	5
S. Wright	st Lockyer b Jackson	1	b Wisden	3
W. Newhall	c Diver b Jackson	5	b Caffyn	6
— Morgan	c Jackson b Parr	0	c Lockyer b Caffyn	0
J. Walker	b Jackson	2	b Wisden	0
W. Crossley	b Parr	0	c Carpenter b Caffyn	4
W. Comery	hit w b Parr	0	l b w b Caffyn	5
R. Bage	b Jackson	3	not out	0
Harry Lillywhite	c Carpenter b Jackson	0	st Lockyer b Caffyn	0
F. Barclay	run out	0	run out	1
— Hallis	not out	0	b Wisden	5
	b 1 l-b 1 w , n-b ,	2	b 1, l-b 3, w , n-b	4
	Total	38	Total	54

Umpires..John Lillywhite and Charles Vinten.

England.	First Innings.		Second Innings.
T. Hayward	b Hallis	33	
R Carpenter	c Senior b Hallis	26	
T. Wisden	run out	3	
G. Parr	b Gibbes	7	
W. Caffyn	b Gibbes	5	
T. Lockyer	c Lang b Hallis	12	
A. Diver	c Hallis b Gibbes	1	
H. H. Stephenson	b Hallis	10	
J. Cæsar	b Hallis	6	
J. Grundy	b Hallis	20	
J. Jackson	not out	8	
	b 10 l-b 1, w 12, n b 2	25	b , l-b , w , n-b
	Total	156	

England won in one innings and 64 runs.

F. Lillywhite's Registered Scoring Books and Sheets may be obtained on the ground.

THE ANALYSIS OF THE BOWLING—*corrected.*

STATES—FIRST INNINGS.

	Balls.	*Runs.*	*M'n Overs.*	*Wickets.*	*Wides.*	*No Balls.*
Parr	116	26	12	9	0	0
Jackson	112	10	19	10	0	0

STATES—SECOND INNINGS.

Wisden	136	24	22	4	0	0
Caffyn	136	26	25	16	0	0

ENGLAND—FIRST INNINGS.

S. Wright	56	20	7	0	0	0
Crossley	4	1	0	0	0	0
Comery	72	31	5	0	1	0
Hallis	173	45	26	6	4	0
Marsh	32	6	4	0	3	1
Gibbes	84	28	9	3	3	0

THE SECOND MATCH, FOR THE BENEFIT OF THE ENGLISH PLAYERS.

LOCKYER *v.* H. H. STEPHENSON'S SIDE *(with five gentlemen each from the States).*

THURSDAY, October 6.

These two celebrated wicket-keepers had agreed to select sides, but excellent as was the play exhibited in the match, we still entertain an impression that a renewal of the contest which took place at Montreal, between The All England and United Elevens, would have proved far more interesting. We merely record the particulars of the score, accompanied by one remark, that the arrangements, *on the part of England,* were most miserably carried out, leaving affairs entirely in the hands of others, whom, we hear, *they have since blamed.* The score stood as follows :—

At Hoboken, New York, October 6th, 7th and 8th, 1859.

Lockyer's side.	First Innings.		Second Innings.	
Wisden	b Hayward	12	b Stephenson	0
Grundy	b Jackson	31	c Diver b Stephenson	4
Caffyn	b Hayward	23	c Lillywhite b Jackson	1
Parr	c Carpenter b Jackson	6	run out	36
Lockyer	b Jackson	1	c Hayward b Stephenson	14
Cæsar	b Stephenson	52	b Jackson	3
R. Waller	b Jackson	1	b Stephenson	12
— Wilby	c & b Stephenson	9	c Jackson b Stephenson	7
H. Wright	c Gibbes b Hayward	10	b Jackson	0
— Hudson	b Hayward	0	not out	0
— Bashford	not out	0	Jackson	1
	b 13, l.b 4, w 1, n-b ,	18	b 2, l-b 3, w 7, n b ,	12
	Total	163	Total	90

Umpires..Mr. C. Vinten and W. Crossley.

Stephenson's side.	First Innings.		Second Innings.	
Sharp	run out	3	c & b Wisden	18
Jackson	c Lockyer b Wisden	25	c Lockyer b Wisden	2
Carpenter	not out	52	c Bashford b Wisden	3
Hayward	c Wilby b Wisden	1	c Caffyn b Wisden	28
Diver	b Grundy	0	not out	18
Gibbes	b Wisden	1	c Lockyer b Wisden	0
H.H.Stephenson	c & b Grundy	1	c H. Wright b Caffyn	3
John Lillywhite	run out	1	c Parr b Wisden	7
Lang	b Grundy	6	c Cæsar b Wisden	0
Ford	b Grundy	0	b Wisden	0
George	b Grundy	1	run out	5
	b , l b 2, w , n b ,	2	b , l b 2, w , n b ,	2
	Total	93	Total	86

ANALYSIS OF THE BOWLING.

LOCKYER'S SIDE—FIRST INNINGS.

	Balls.	*Runs.*	*M'n Overs.*	*Wickets.*	*Wides.*	*No Balls.*
Jackson	121	55	11	4	1	0
Hayward	164	64	16	4	0	0
Stephenson	50	26	4	2	0	0

SECOND INNINGS.

	Balls.	*Runs.*	*M'n Overs.*	*Wickets.*	*Wides.*	*No Balls.*
Jackson	120	28	17	4	0	0
Hayward	68	21	9	0	0	0
Stephenson	56	29	0	5	7	0

ANALYSIS OF BOWLING *continued—*

STEPHENSON'S SIDE—FIRST INNINGS.

	Balls.	*Runs.*	*M'n Overs.*	*Wickets.*	*Wides.*	*No Balls.*
Caffyn....	40	23	1	0	0	0
Wisden....	140	47	17	3	0	0
Grundy....	107	21	15	5	0	0
SECOND INNINGS.						
Wisden....	114	45	13	8	0	0
Grundy....	40	14	6	0	0	0
Caffyn.....	72	25	7	1	0	0

This finished the week's cricketing at New York, which, no doubt will give an impulse to the noble game, as a scientific and healthful outdoor manly exercise. During our sojourn we were invited to the Racket Court, on Thirteenth Street, and saw several good games played, and it is quite likely that, ere long, our champion player will be showing his prowess in that establishment.

THE DINNER TO THE ENGLISH PARTY.

On the Friday evening a splendid dinner was given at the Astor House, to the English party, by the St. George's Club. The banquet was in the Ladies' Ordinary, which was very tastefully fitted up, the flags of the St. George's Club being at the head of the room. The dinner was got up in a style which fully sustained the high reputation which the Astor House has always held on similar occasions; mine host, Stetson, winning renewed expressions of approbation from all who partook of this *recherché* affair. The dinner consisted of the usual variety, and a great abundance of everything in season.

Mr. R. Waller, President of the Club, was in the chair.

The President opened the proceedings in a neat speech, in which he alluded to the fact that the Spartans were famed for out-door games. Indeed, he believed that the noble and manly game of cricket was traceable to these people. He, however, would not now argue that point, but requested the company to fill to the first toast, which was "The noble and manly game of Cricket."

The toast was received with three times three, and the band played "Rule Britannia" and the "Star-spangled Banner."

The President then stated that the Queen's health was received with enthusiasm, not only by Englishmen but by Americans, for her exemplary conduct as a wife and mother. He gave, "The Queen, God bless her."

Three times three and one cheer more greeted this sentiment, and the Glee Club sang "God save the Queen," the whole company standing and joining in the chorus.

The President then said that this free and enlightened country demanded respect from all, whether aliens or citizens. He was sure, therefore, that the company would do honour to their chief magistrate He gave "The President of the United States."

Nine cheers were given for the President, and the band played "Hail, Columbia," the company all standing.

John Brougham here being called on for a comic song, said, "Mr. President, with pleasure." He then gave, what appeared a version of his own, "The Rale Ould Irish Gentleman," with such a funny brogue, as to keep the company in a roar of laughter during the whole time he was singing. He was warmly applauded.

The President, in introducing the fourth toast, spoke of the rapid strides cricket had made in England during the last century. He alluded to several cricketers, including Hiran, Ward, Lord Frederick Beauclerk, &c. Ward made the longest score,* and remained longer in than any man who ever played; and Lord Beauclerk was bowled out by a ratcatcher. The President also gave a history of the All England Eleven, out of which arose the United All England Eleven, and to these clubs they were indebted for the pleasure of the company of the gentlemen who were at the table that evening. He called attention to the fact that these men, many of whom had never been at sea before, had come three thousand miles to play a game of cricket, and he trusted that soon these international games would become general, so that billiards and chess, of which the champions were in New York—(applause)—and rackets, would also have their representatives from England. He gave "The English Eleven—our guests to-night."

The customary nine cheers were given for the guests, and Mr. Phillips sung "The Englishman."

---

* This, we may add, is not correct. A person by the name of Adams of Saffron Waldron, in Essex, scored 279—one more.—F. L.

Mr. George Parr very briefly returned thanks on behalf of the English.

A Gentleman referred in flattering terms to Mr. Stevens, on whose grounds the match was played, and after some able remarks on the game in general, and his own prowess in the old country, and a compliment to Mr. Lillywhite (whom he supposed to be an ancestor of those at the recent match), he concluded by hoping that balls would continue to fly between the two countries with the rapidity, but not the hostility, of cannon balls, and that cricketers on each side would exert themselves to do what was best for their country, so that they would soon establish peace on earth, and goodwill towards men. He offered the following sentiment:—"England and America—the mother and the daughter. One race, one language, one interest, one hope. Those whom God hath joined together let not man dare to put asunder."

The party, after enjoying a most convivial meeting, retired at somewhat a late hour.

THE MATCH AT PHILADELPHIA.

We left for this city by the Saturday night's train from New York (Oct. 8), and did the ninety miles in about three hours, arriving at midnight at the Girard House Hotel, where the reception was most enthusiastic. Refreshments were duly provided by the worthy, and soonwe found most liberal, proprietors of the hotel (being introduced first to Mr. H. A. Chadwick), whose attention to us was all that could be needed. The usual preliminaries of securing the keys of the bedrooms having been accomplished, and a considerable amount of conversation about the events of the forthcoming match, all retired to rest.

SUNDAY, October 9,

having been religiously kept (cricket not having been mentioned), all were "eager for the fray" on

MONDAY, October 10.

The ground is situate on the Carnac estate, about two miles and a half from the centre of the city, and is easily accessible per railway passing through the streets. Upon our arrival on the ground, we found that preparations had been made for the reception of the Eleven, quite equal to those of the St. George's Club, at Hoboken. It had, however, been raining all night and during the morning, the ground, therefore, was dreadfully wet; so much so, that it appeared almost like a sheet of water, and it was past two o'clock before any of the English Cricketers could make their appearance, but it was even then too wet to proceed with the contest, notwithstanding the anxiety of the Americans to be at work. About half-past three o'clock, Hammond (of Maidstone, Kent,) and Tom Senior, who were the caterers on the ground, having secured a couple of waggon loads of sawdust, arrangements were made to commence; but very little, of course, was accomplished on that day—nine wickets only falling for 41 runs—as the stumps were drawn at half-past five o'clock. No play took place on

TUESDAY, October 11,

owing to an election in the city!!

WEDNESDAY, October 12.

Great excitement had prevailed during the previous day and evening. This was a splendid morning; the sun shone brightly, with a blue sky, and the temperature just cool enough to realise what is called in England "a jolly cricketing day." At half-past ten o'clock the English party left the Girard House, and upon arriving on the ground found a very large company to meet them, with a number of the young Americans practising in all parts of the ground; the band, too, was playing "God save the Queen," as the English entered amidst most enthusiastic cheering. In two more hours the ground presented a most animated appearance. We never saw such a magnificent sight; about one thousand ladies were seated by themselves, and they appeared to be just as enthusiastic in their demonstrations of applause as if they had been versed in all the mysteries of the game. And if any additional incentive had been required to induce the English Eleven to exhibit their skill to the greatest advantage, it was afforded by the presence of so large and beautiful an assemblage of the fair sex. They certainly order these matters in America, *as far as regards appearances,* infinitely better than we do, for nothing could present a more delightful aspect than the collection together of so large a number of American ladies, seated by themselves, tastefully dressed in every variety of modern costume, and forming, by the combination of the colours of their dresses and the attractiveness of their countenances, one of the most delightful pictures that the eye of man could rest upon. It seems to be the rule in the "*United States,*" that, on large public occasions, the ladies and gentlemen should be, as it were, *dis-united.* We, as Englishmen, should raise our voices against such a custom ; but, *chacun à son goût.* The effect, however, was unquestionably, "*tarnation good.*"

We may here add, that LILLYWHITE'S *Guide to Cricketers* did much service to all ignorant on points of the game. *Bell's Life in London,* in their report of this match, had occasion to call the attention of their readers to the excellence of this Twenty-two, and remarked, that they were the best yet seen by the English Cricketers, to the truth of which opinion we can add our hearty concurrence. They showed some excellent points in the way of fielding, and were justly applauded by their opponents for the skill they displayed. And we should be inclined to think that, with good bowlers, they possess, in other respects, the materials for making good cricketers, as it was quite evident, during the progress of the game, that it is a recreation into which they can enter with spirit, and contest with great energy. Parr being unwell, Mr. Ellis kindly officiated as umpire, while Julius Cæsar was his substitute in the field. The English were most hospitably entertained here by the gentlemen of the Twenty-two, who, after the match was concluded, very kindly gave them a free benefit, paying *all expenses* that were incurred.* The final score stood as follows, the Eleven winning by seven wickets :

* Had judicious management, however, been forthcoming on the part of the English, they would have realized a large sum of money !

CORRECT SCORE

FROM F. LILLYWHITE'S PRINTING TENT
OF LORD'S & KENNINGTON OVAL LONDON.

At Philadelphia, Eleven of England *v.* Twenty-two of the United States.

Monday and Wednesday, October 10th and 12th, 1859.

Twenty-two.	First Innings.		Second Innings.	
J. Lang	b Parr	2	c Lockyer b Grundy	0
C. B. Sarratt	b Jackson	0	b Grundy	1
W. R. Wister	b Wisden	9	b Grundy	3
A. C. Barclay	b Jackson	0	c Wisden	3
W. Newhall	c Parr	3	c & b Wisden	0
W. Hammond	c Grundy b Parr	0	c & b Wisden	0
A. H. Gibbes	b Caffyn	20	b Grundy	6
H. Wright	b Parr	1	c Stephenson b Jackson	7
T. M. Hall	h w b Caffyn	3	run out	0
W. Wilby	b Caffyn	0	b Jackson	0
C. H. T. Collis	b Jackson	0	st Lockyer b Wisden	0
T. Sentor	b Jackson	3	b Wisden	6
C. Vernon	c Cæsar b Jackson	5	run out	2
— Kephart	b Jackson	0	run out	10
S. Wright	st Lockyer b Carpenter	3	c & b Wisden	2
W. Morgan	c Lockyer b Carpen er	9	b Jackson	3
E. C. Hunt	c Caffyn b Jackson	1	l b w Jaekson	0
C. M. Bayrard	c Caffyn b Carpenter	1	c Carpenter b Wisden	0
J. Wister	run out	19	b Jackson	5
H. Fisher	b Jackson	4	b Jackson	2
W. Hallis	not out	7	c Jackson b Wisden	9
A. Waterman	c Carpenter b Caffyn	0	not out	0
	b 4 l-b w , n-b ,	4	b , l-b 2, w , n-b	2
	Total	94	Total	60

Umpires--Cæsar and H. Sharp.

England.	First Innings.		Second Innings.	
T. Hayward	c Wilby b H. Wright	34	c Lang b Kephart	0
H. Carpenter	c Gibbes b Senior	22	c Hammond b Senior	7
A. Diver	b H. Wright	2		
W. Caffyn	b Senior	4	not out	6
T. Lockyer	not out	31	st Barclay b Lang	9
J. Grundy	c Newhall b Senior	5	not out	2
H.H Stephenson	b Senior	1		
John Lillywhite	b Senior	0		
J. Wisden	b Gibbes	3		
J. Jackson	c W. Wister b Senior	6		
G. Parr(sick)				
	b 4 l-b 3, w 11, n-b ,	18	b , l-b , w 4, n-b 1	5
	Total	126	Total	29

ANALYSIS OF THE BOWLING—*corrected.*

(From F. Lillywhite's *Registered Scoring Book.*)

	Balls.	Runs.	M'n overs.	Wickets.	Wides.	No Balls.
STATES—FIRST INNINGS.						
Parr	144	18	23	4	0	0
Carpenter	44	9	4	3	0	0
Jackson	236	37	40	8	0	0
Wisden	32	2	6	1	0	0
Caffyn	82	24	10	4	0	0
SECOND INNINGS.						
Jackson	64	7	10	6	0	0
Wisden	157	39	20	8	0	0
Grundy	92	12	16	4	0	0
ENGLAND—FIRST INNINGS.						
Hallis	120	25	16	0	3	0
Senior	105	20	12	6	5	0
Gibbs	100	32	10	1	2	0
Waterman	68	17	10	0	0	0
H. Wright	56	14	7	2	1	0
SECOND INNINGS.						
Senior	23	7	2	1	0	1
Rephardt	16	5	1	1	1	0
Wilby	24	7	2	0	3	0
Lang	12	5	1	1	0	0

George Parr, who began playing in the above match, was, after the first day's play, compelled to keep to his bed. He was hit on the elbow, by Jackson, at the second match at New York, which having been somewhat too lightly regarded, began to swell fearfully; so much so that, at one time, it became a question whether it would not be judicious for him to go at once to Montreal, and there await the arrival of his comrades, after they had "polished off" their remaining opponents. He, however, gradually got better.

At the conclusion of the above match the Eleven were most enthusiastically cheered, and the Twenty-two were highly pleased in having made so, good a stand against such a formidable "team." It may also be stated, that the majority of the Twenty-two were self-taught cricketers, being principally Americans, and great credit is therefore due, both to themselves and Hammond, their professional. They are excellent managers, will be good cricketers, and are really good and spirited fellows. This was the opinion of the majority of the English party. We were most hospitably entertained, not only by the gentlemen comprising the club, but by the worthy proprietors of the Girard House Hotel, to whose establishment we can safely recommend any one desirous of paying a visit to the liberal citizens of Philadelphia. We had omitted to state, that during the match we had to deplore the loss of our valuable and esteemed friend, Mr. Pickering, he being compelled to return for a few days to Montreal. We had, however, among us our excellent "guide," Mr. Baker, of Ottawa, who had never flinched from his work from the time we landed at Quebec; he was ever ready to lend one assistance, and we sincerely trust that he may afford us an opportunity of returning his kindness by paying an early visit to Old England. A more enthusiastic and true lover of the noble game of cricket never existed. We have now before us his original notes and figures, as scored in LILLYWHITE'S *Registered Scoring Book*,* which was placed in his (Mr. Baker's) hands for the purpose. A somewhat singular incident occurred in this match—*Carpenter being caught off a "wide ball,"* erroneously called by the States umpire. According to some of our best judges in England, he should have been given "out," but it was decided, at the time, that he was "not out," and he consequently remained.†

In order to publish the whole particulars of what took place during our absence from England, we give the score of the "Benefit Match," which the Philadelphians had so kindly arranged on behalf of the English Cricketers. It was five of the NORTH and five of the SOUTH of England, assisted by six Americans on each side. The score stood thus:—

---

* F. LILLYWHITE'S Registered Books for 50, 25, and 12 Matches, as well as Single Score Sheets, may be had of him at 15, Kennington Oval, per post, or of Piper & Co., Paternoster Row, and at all wholesale houses, Cricket-bat makers, &c. LILLYWHITE'S GUIDE, price 1s.; post-free, 1s. 1d.

† On which subject see "Interpretation of Laws," in "LILLYWHITE'S *Guide*," for 1860, assisted by the Author of the "Cricket Field," and other well-known authorities.

SOUTH OF ENGLAND—First Innings.

Caffyn, b Grundy	10
Lillywhite, b Grundy	8
Lockyer, c Jackson b. Hayward	9
Stephenson, c Collis b Grundy	3
Wisden, c Barclay b Grundy	10
Davis, c Carpenter b Grundy	9
J. Wister, b Grundy	3
Stevens, c Carpenter b Grundy	2
Howe, b Hayward	0
Johnson, c Jackson b Hayward	5
G. Newhall, not out	0
Total	59

NORTH OF ENGLAND—First Innings.

Diver, b Wisden	6
Jackson, c Stevens b Lillywhite	60
Carpenter, st Stephenson b. Lillywhite	34
Grundy, c Stevens b Lockyer	14
Newhall, not out	4
Barclay, c Wisden b Lockyer	1
Barlow, not out	0
Hayward, Kuhn, Henry, and Collis not in.	
Wide, 1	1
Total	120

The play was stopped in the afternoon in consequence of the rain. The North played splendidly. There were about 2,000 persons on the ground.

Soon after the above match the Cricketers proceeded to the Girard House, where a grand dinner was given to them the same evening; and the interest manifested for the progress of the game, during the entertainment, as evinced by the very excellent and genuine speeches delivered, is a sufficient proof that "Cricket in Philadelphia" has every prospect of becoming a national game. We now, with very much regret, took leave of the citizens of Philadelphia, and on

THE BREAK DOWN IN A SNOW STORM.

FOUR HORSE BUSS.

SATURDAY AFTERNOON, October 15,

proceeded by train to Buffalo, *en route* to Hamilton, C.W. Of this journey we are unable to report very favourably, as it was both tedious and disagreeable. Change of cars occurred at almost every stopping place, and nothing was forthcoming to satisfy the inner man until we reached the village of Avon, at 8h 30m on Sunday morning, where a hurried breakfast was provided. On our arrival at Buffalo, we found the train for the Falls had departed, and we had therefore no other resource but to take a land conveyance for the Falls, if we desired to keep our engagement at Hamilton, and see anything of the world-renowned Niagara. The 22 miles between Buffalo and the Falls were crossed in five hours! and by tea-time we found ourselves safely housed in the International Hotel, on the American side, which is, without doubt, the finest hotel we have yet visited. Here, to our great delight, we met Mr. Pickering again. Our detention at Buffalo deprived us of much anticipated pleasure in viewing this celebrated wonder of nature. We nevertheless spent all our spare moments on Monday morning in seeing the more prominent points of interest on the American side, but unfortunately our time did not permit us to visit the Canada side. Having thus spent three hours (from six to nine, a.m.) at the Falls, we were compelled to leave for Hamilton, C.W., and at 10 a.m. we passed over the wonderful Niagara Suspension Bridge, which spans the river about two miles distance below the Falls. It is a noble and stupendous structure, and the work of Mr. John A. R. Roebling, of Trenton, New Jersey, being commenced in 1852. Formerly the bridge here was of much smaller dimensions. It was begun in 1849, by Mr. Charles Elliot, who first crossed it in an iron basket, slung under a single cable of iron wire. Afterwards, many people crossed it in this way, being let down the incline, and drawn up on the opposite side by a windlass. While six workmen were employed on the footpath of this bridge, a terrific gale burst upon them, tore the planks away, and left four of their number clinging to two thin wires, which swung fearfully to and fro, while the whirling rapids raged beneath them; the other two escaped on fragments of board to the shore. A brave comrade descended in the basket during a lull in the gale, and by means of a ladder rescued his companions from their awful position. This basket is still preserved on the Canada side. The bridge, of which we give an engraving, is of enormous strength, and forms a communication between Canada and the States, over which the cars of the Great Western and the New York Central Railway Companies run without causing the slightest vibration. The cost of its construction was 500,000 dollars (more than £100,000 sterling). Steam carriages first crossed on March 8, 1855. The road for carriages is suspended 28 feet below the railway line. The following statistics of this enormous bridge will, no doubt, be interesting:—The height of the towers on the American side is 88 feet; those on the Canada side are 78 feet high; length of bridge is 800 feet; width, 24 feet; height above the river, 250 feet! There are four enormous wire cables, each of about 10 inches diameter, which contain 4,000 miles of wire, and the ultimate capacity of the four cables is about 12,400 tons! The total weight of the bridge is 800 tons, and it combines, in an eminent degree, strength with elegance of structure. Our engraving is from a photograph.

In two hours, or a little more, we were welcomed to Hamilton by an immense crowd—all eager to see "those who had come from England," and had so recently beaten with ease three successive Twenty-twos, with every apparent probability of adding a fourth victory to that number.

The sight at the station we can scarcely describe. It was well known, for many miles around, that we could arrive by no other train than this, and it was with great difficulty we could emerge from our cars to get out of the station.

Upon our arrival over the suspension bridge (where all the baggage is examined), we received the greatest courtesy from the Custom-house authorities, which the English party did not fail to appreciate. We should have liked to have made our special acknowledgments to our "worthy friend," but time would not permit of asking even a question, especially as the printing apparatus was left behind at Buffalo, although *expected* to join us at this spot. In this, however, we were disappointed, and were obliged to proceed without it; no printing, consequently, could take place at Hamilton.

ARRIVAL AT HAMILTON.

ARRIVAL AT HAMILTON RAILWAY STATION.

MONDAY, October 17.

Unlike some of the bright days enjoyed in the cities of Montreal, New York, and Philadelphia, the weather in Hamilton was cold and threatening; so much so, that grave doubts were entertained of the game proceeding; but, in spite of this state of affairs, we got to work at 3 p.m. England having won the toss, took the field. The wickets were very fair, but owing to the wretched state of the weather, a great deal of rain having fallen in the night, they did not play as well as we anticipated. On

TUESDAY, October 18,

the weather was worse, if possible, being showery and extremely cold, and therefore but little cricket can be chronicled. An immense assemblage, however, were in attendance, and, notwithstanding the weather, the scene was far more lively than one could possibly have expected. The printing tent was visible this morning, and excited much public attention when the statement of the game was issued from the press. Messrs. Pickering, Dykes, and Gillespy played exceedingly well for their respective scores of 10, 10, and 9 The wicket-keeping of Lockyer—as in all the previous matches—was quite astonishing, exceeding, if possible, anything that he has accomplished in England; he was frequently applauded, and such was the effect of his performances upon the spectators, it was *not believed, by many*, that the ball had *ever been delivered, and returned to the bowler again!!*

WEDNESDAY, October 19.

No improvement in the weather, except, indeed, that it was somewhat colder. It will be seen by the subjoined score, that the Twenty-two put the Eleven in for 41 runs, which was accomplished by the two first wickets—Jackson and Caffyn—they thus proving victorious by nine wickets, and deciding numerous bets made in England with regard to the Eleven winning all their four matches, for which purpose they left this country. The English put up at Mr. Rice's, the Anglo-American Hotel. The umpire for the Twenty-two was the worthy President of the Club, R. N. Law, Esq.

CORRECT SCORE

FROM F. LILLYWHITE'S PRINTING TENT OF LORD'S & KENNINGTON OVAL LONDON.

At Hamilton, Eleven of England *v.* Twenty-two of Upper Canada.

Monday, Tuesday, and Wednesday, October 17th, 18th, and 19th, 1859.

Twenty-two.	First Innings.	Second Innings.	
Starling, b Stephenson	2	run out	3
T. Phillips, c Cæsar b Stephenson	5	c Carpenter b Wisden	4
Bayley, b Grundy	0	b Wisden	0
Harris, b Grundy	0	b Wisden	5
Worswick, b Grundy	2	c Carpenter b Wisden	0
Rykert, b Grundy	0	l b w b Grundy	2
Parsons, b Stephenson	3	c Carpenter b Grundy	10
Heward, b Stephenson	3	c Carpenter b Wisden	1
Reid, b Grundy	0	b Wisden	5
W. Totten, b Grundy	0	c Diver b Wisden	0
Rogerson, c Lillywhite b Grundy	0	st Lockyer b Wisden	0
Dykes, run out	10	b Wisden	4
Jones, b Stephenson	2	b Grundy	1
W. Pickering, b Jackson	10	b Grundy	2
Bosteed, l b w b Stephenson	0	run out	3
Stokes, c Lockyer b Stephenson	0	not out	0
Sharp, c Diver b Wisden	9	c Carpenter b Wisden	3
Gillespy, b. Jackson	0	b Wisden	0
H. Totten, b Jackson	0	b Wisden	1
Hamilton, b Jackson	1	b Wisden	5
Despard, not out	9	c Lockyer b Wisden	0
O'Reilly, b Wisden	6	c Lockyer b Grundy	1
B 3 l b 1	4	B 1, l b 2	3
Total	66	Total	53

ENGLAND.

First Innings.		Second Innings.	
T. Hayward, b. Rogerson	14		
R. Carpenter, c Heward b Parsons	2		
A. Diver, b Rogerson	11		
W. Caffyn, c Harris b Parsons	25	not out	16
J. Grundy, run out	2		
T. Lockyer, run out	1		
J. Cæsar, b Sharp	6		
John Lillywhite, c Stokes b Parsons	6		
J. Wisden, b Sharp	0		
H. H. Stephenson, b Sharp	0		
J. Jackson, not out	0	not out	17
B 7, l b 2, w 3	12	B 1, l b 3, w 4	8
Total	79	Total	41

ANALYSIS OF THE BOWLING.

CANADIANS—FIRST INNINGS.

	Balls.	Runs.	M'n Overs.	Wickets.	Wides.
Grundy	124	22	23	7	0
Stephenson	120	19	19	7	0
Jackson	68	2	15	4	0
Wisden	66	19	5	2	0

SECOND INNINGS.

	Balls.	Runs.	M'n Overs.	Wickets.	Wides.
Wisden	180	24	27	14	0
Jackson	40	11	5	0	0
Grundy	136	15	24	5	0

ENGLAND—FIRST INNINGS.

	Balls.	Runs.	M'n Overs.	Wickets.	Wides.
Rogerson	76	34	5	1	3
Sharp	37	5	5	3	0
Parsons	112	28	13	4	1

SECOND INNINGS.

	Balls.	Runs.	M'n Overs.	Wickets.	Wides.
Sharp	40	20	3	0	1
Parsons	36	13	2	0	0
Rogerson	4	1	0	0	1

THURSDAY, October 20.

Some cricket, this day, was attempted for a Benefit Match, but the weather being intensely cold, the play excited so little interest, that the game was, consequently, discontinued. Amidst the hearty cheers of the Hamiltonians, the English party left that evening for Rochester, U.S., where, after travelling 210 miles, they arrived on

FRIDAY MORNING, October 21.

This was an extra match, and arranged at New York, but not being included in the number which the Eleven undertook to play, it was of course necessary to obtain the permission of the parties by whom they had been engaged. Immense excitement prevailed, but owing to the continued coldness of the weather little could be done in the shape of showing what cricket was; in fact, the umpire ought to have pronounced it as unfit for playing the game. Great preparations had been made and the expenses of the contest were borne by a few spirited gentlemen connected with the club. The match, however, from this cause, was a failure, and proved, we fear, a heavy loss to the promoters. This day the Eleven got the Twenty two out for 39 runs, themselves only losing two wickets for 35 runs. On

SATURDAY, October 22,

no play took place, owing to a heavy fall of snow, but a game of base-ball was got up among the players of that game and a portion of the English party, and which took place on the base-ball ground, about a mile from the cricket ground. The latter is situated about two miles from the town, and had been enclosed at a great expense, for the occasion. The base-ball game is somewhat similar to the English game of "rounders," as played by school-boys ; but the judgment displayed by the base-ball players was especially conspicuous over that of the English cricketers, who, no doubt, however, would soon have been able to compete with their more experienced opponents at their "own game." Caffyn played exceedingly well, but the English thought catching the ball the *first bound* a very childish game.

SUNDAY, October 23.

The whole of the party made a trip of 140 miles to the Niagara Falls and back, where they spent the Sunday, and were thus enabled to repair their previous disappointment by visiting the Falls on the Canadian side. The Falls may be justly classed among the wonders of the world. They are the pride of America, and unequalled in magnitude and grandeur by any other known cataract. It is impossible to describe the delight with which the Eleven gazed upon that tumultuous crash of water. The Horse Shoe, or Canadian Fall, is 2000 feet wide, and 154 feet high. The roar of the Falls can, it is said, be heard occasionally at a distance of twenty miles, but that must, of course, depend upon the direction and strength of the wind. The mist has been seen nearly fifty miles off. Over this magnificent precipice the irresistible tide rushes at the rate of one hundred million tons of water every hour! The stream here is about three-quarters of a mile wide, and it was close to this spot that Blonden went over on a rope in the presence of thousands of spectators.

NIAGARA FALLS.

HORSE SHOE FALL.

TABLE ROCK, NIAGARA FALLS.

WHIRLPOOL—NIAGARA FALLS.

TERRAPIN TOWER, NIAGARA FALLS.

The Falls of Niagara were first seen by a white man 180 years ago. A charge of twenty-five cents is made as you enter the toll on the Island, and each visitor has his name entered in a book, after which he is entitled to pass as often as he pleases during the year. The Terrapin Tower, 45 feet high (see engraving of the Horse Shoe Fall), commands a magnificent view of Niagara, and where will be found, cut out, the names of nearly all the English cricketers. Having thus seen all that could be seen in the time allotted to us, we returned, per rail, to Rochester. The day was beautifully fine, and never will October the 23rd be forgotten by the Cricketers of England.

MONDAY, October 24,

the match was resumed, but the weather was unmistakeably cold. The score will show that, on

TUESDAY, October 25,

the match was brought to a conclusion in favour of England in one innings and 68 runs—thus *winning all the matches played.* This Twenty-two was a mixture of players of the States and Canada, many of whom had before met the Eleven in their previous contests. The match, therefore, was entitled "Twenty-two of the United States and Canada." Hayward and Carpenter again exhibited a good display of batting, as they had done in previous matches, and it will be seen that the slow bowling of Wisden was very destructive. The players had to field in muffs and greatcoats, and such was the cold they could scarcely feel the handle of the bat, or know whether they had fielded the ball or not; indeed, such cricketing weather, had never before been experienced. It was really like playing a match in the depth of winter; and the batsman very appropriately exclaimed, when his wicket was lowered by a ball from Wisden's end—"*Shiver* my timbers, I'm out." The most agreeable innings on such a day could only be obtained in-doors with a hot dinner before you, and a bottle of old Port to follow. We now append the score of this "Frosty Match," but not without expressing the hope that we may never witness such another :—

CORRECT SCORE

FROM F. LILLYWHITE'S PRINTING TENT OF LORD'S & KENNINGTON OVAL LONDON.

At Rochester, U.S., Eleven of England *v.* Twenty-two of the United States and Canada, Friday, Monday, and Tuesday, October 21, 24, and 25, 1859.

Twenty-two.	First Innings.		Second Innings.	
W. Hammond	c Carpenter b Wisden	4	b Wisden	6
Sharp	st Lockyer b Wisden	0	b Jackson	4
D. S. Booth	b Wisden	1	st Lockyer b Jackson	0
Beatty	st. Lockyer b Wisden	2	b Wisden	0
H. Wright	b Jackson	13	b Jackson	1
Capt. Hammond	run out	2	c and b Wisden	0
Capt. K. Hugesson	b Wisden	2	b Jackson	3
Machattie	c and b Wisden	0	st Lockyer b Wisden	1
Pickering	run out	11	not out	14
Stephenson	b Wisden	0	absent	0
J. Higham	st Lockyer b Wisden	0	c Carpenter b Jackson	0
T. Senior	b Jackson	1	b Wisden	8
A. Jackson	b Wisden	0	st Lockyer b Wisden	0
Collis	b Jackson	0	st Lockyer b Wisden	4
Tarrant	b Wisden	0	b Wisden	2
Crossley	not out	3	c Carpenter b Wisden	0
Hines	b Wisden	0	b Wisden	4
G. Tarrant	b Wisden	0	b Jackson	2
H. Lillywhite	c Carpenter b Wisden	0	b Wisden	0
Wm. Collis	b Wisden	0	absent	0
Hallis	c Lockyer b Wisden	0	c Carpenter b Wisden	9
Pattison	c Cæsar b Wisden	0	c Jackson b Wisden	0
			b 1 l-b 2 w 1	4
	Total	39	Total	62

Umpires, Mr. W. Baker, of Ottawa, and Smith, of Utica.

England.	First Innings.		Second Innings.
W. Caffyn	c Hammond b Hallis	14	
J. Jackson	run out	12	
T. Hayward	c Hallis b Crossley	50	
R. Carpenter	c Hines b Senior	18	
J. Grundy	c Higham b Pickering	8	
T. Lockyer	c Hallis b Wright	19	
A. Diver	c Hines b Machattie	6	
John Lillywhite	b Wright	4	
J. Cæsar	st Higham b Machattie	11	
J. Wisden	c Lillywhite b Machattie	2	
H. H. Stephenson	not out	1	
	b 6 w 20	26	
Total		171	

ANALYSIS OF THE BOWLING.

(From F. Lillywhite's *Registered Scoring Book.)*

STATES AND CANADA—FIRST INNINGS.

	Balls.	Runs.	M'n Overs.	Wickets.	Wides.	No Balls.
Wisden.........	72	17	7	16	0	0
Jackson........	68	22	10	3	0	0
SECOND INNINGS.						
Wisden.........	89	43	4	13	0	0
Jackson........	84	17	13	6	1	0
ENGLAND—FIRST INNINGS.						
Hallis..........	136	46	12	1	5	0
Sharp..........	8	16	0	0	0	0
Senior.........	68	17	8	1	5	0
Crossley........	20	2	4	0	4	0
Pickering......	48	21	3	1	3	0
H. Wright......	48	35	2	3	2	0
Machattie......	36	8	4	3	1	0

The remainder of the day was spent in a match at base-ball, which was got up with a view to lessen the severe loss of the promoters of the cricket match. Notwithstanding the severity of the weather, a goodly sprinkling of the lovers of the game attended to witness it. The names of the players were:—

Oriel, c.
Hutchinson, p.
Diver, 1st b.
Hines, 2nd b.
Lillywhite, 3rd b.
Baker, s. s.
Sullivan, r. f.
Stewart, c. f.
Grundy, l. f.

Lockyer, c.
Willis, p.
Cæsar, s. s.
Putman, 1st b.
H. Stephenson, 2nd b.
Ives, 3rd b.
Hammond, r. f.
Collis, c. f.
Beardsley, l. f.

According to good judges of the game present, the English cricketers played remarkably well, and Lockyer's playing "behind the bat" could not have been surpassed. At the conclusion of the game, the whole party made way that evening for Montreal. We arrived at Rome on

WEDNESDAY MORNING, October 26,

at half-past two o'clock, a distance of 145 miles, and soon found that, "when at Rome you must do as Rome does." We immediately adjourned to the American Hotel, where we were greeted with the not very pleasing intelligence that there were "no beds". The annexed engraving will represent the Cricketers during their four hours' stay, awaiting a train for Cape St. Vincent, from whence we proceeded in a river boat, going up a canal cut for the purpose, and just about the width of the boat itself. We soon arrived at Kingston, a magnificent view of which place we obtained on the water, previous to getting to the wharf.

The scene at Rome was a most uncomfortable but laughable one; some were lying on the floor, with portmanteaus and carpet-bags for pillows, and a rug or a great-coat for a covering. In this manner the Cricketers of England were dispersed over all parts of the office. The landlord of the hotel was exceedingly obliging and attentive, and did as much for us as these circumstances admitted, for although he had no sleeping accommodation he gave us a good breakfast before starting at six o'clock. We arrived at Cape St. Vincent, from whence we proceeded to Kingston, where we ascertained that the train to Montreal *was then due* at the station, nearly four miles distant. Mr. Baker and others instantly proceeded to the station per trap, for the purpose, if possible, of stopping the train until the enormous quantity of baggage could be got across. By the extreme kindness of Mr. J. Thompson, the civil and obliging conductor on the Grand Trunk Railway Company, this was effected, the train being kept *waiting an hour,* during which time Messrs. Pickering, Diver, and F. Lillywhite were (very disagreeably) in charge of a "dray" load of baggage. This was a fearful task to perform. The dust was ankle-deep, and the baggage not being strapped, portmanteaus, bags, hat-boxes, &c., were continually tumbling off the said "dray" into the road. With one on each side and the other behind the "brewer's dray," we managed to arrive at the railway station, so much fatigued as to be almost ready to drop, and literally covered with dust. Our appearance caused much merriment among the passengers—as well as our own party—as we stepped foot on the platform; but had we not persevered we should have

NOCTURNAL ENCAMPMENT.

CROSSING FROM KINGSTON WHARF TO RAILWAY STATION.

EMBARKATION FOR ENGLAND.

MEETING OF THE NORTH BRITON AND NOVA SCOTIAN.

had to have remained at Kingston until the following mid-day, as only one train a day left for Montreal. The engraving will represent the difficulties in crossing from Kingston Wharf to the Railway Station, with pickets in charge of baggage—the train waiting for the same.

We were now fairly *en route* for Montreal, which we reached shortly after ten o'clock that night, not at all sorry to again encounter the hospitality at the St. Lawrence Hall.

THURSDAY, October 27,

was spent in settling and arranging matters—such as getting rid of the American coin for English, packing up, and preparing for the voyage home, &c. &c.

FRIDAY, October 28.

A portion of the party went to the steeple-chases, at which the Governor-General (the Hero of Kars) with his suite were present. One of the proprietors of the St. Lawrence Hall rode and won a race. The weather was very cold, and the Canadian winter, in this quarter, evidently setting in. At ten o'clock, p.m., we started per rail for Quebec, where we arrived at six o'clock in the morning. Went immediately across to the tug awaiting passengers for the *North Briton*, Capt. M'Master, where all safely arrived, to again encounter the "deep, deep sea." A great many officers from the garrison were present, to bid us farewell, and at ten o'clock, on

SATURDAY, October 29,

we weighed anchor, and made a move for Old England. Of course everything was pleasant and comfortable until we got out of the 700 miles of river. About 200 miles up the river we met the *Nova Scotian*, which had taken us out, and as we all felt assured that the officers and crew, and probably many of the passengers, would be anxious to know the result of our matches—for they only knew of the first one—Capt. M'Master very kindly gave directions for a large board to be brought on deck, on which was chalked in large letters, "Won all matches." This announcement was read as we passed that noble ship, and followed with deafening cheers from all on board of her. Capt. Boreland, Mr. Macdonald, the purser, and others, were distinctly seen on the bridge, waving their caps in honour of our success. We responded, by giving them such hearty cheers as only can proceed from English throats. Thus we parted; the opposite engraving represents the interesting and exciting scene. We went on charmingly until November 3, when in the evening of that day we had again to encounter the "bumpy" ground, which evidently had not been *rolled* since we left it two months previously. The weather continued fearfully bad—worse than that we experienced in our voyage over—until Sunday, November 6, when the sea lowered about 12 o'clock a.m., but still a head wind. It was, however, only for a short time that the gale subsided, when it came with more terrific force. Poor Caffyn! Away goes the jib-boom!

We very much lament to state that during this gale a sad accident occurred, which resulted in the death of a poor sailor, 63 years of age. He died from the injuries that he then received as we were making fast at Liverpool Dock. Captain M'Master, with the second mate, Mr. Cain, were, with the crew, all forward, in order to save the broken jib-boom from getting entangled with the screw. Frequently the whole body of them were under the gigantic waves, but still the work was to be done, although, unhappily, it could not be accomplished without the loss of life. A sea lifted one of the immense anchors, at the same time knocking the poor fellow underneath it, thus crushing both legs, breaking them across the calves. With all the attention the doctor could bestow, he was never restored to consciousness, and lingered only till we reached England. Whilst the poor sufferer lay in this hopeless state, a subscription was started by Fred. Lillywhite, who, with the able assistance of the Cricketers, the purser, and the passengers generally, collected a sum of £30 16*s*. One gentleman—Mr. Hodges—gave a handsome donation of twenty dollars; Capt. M'Master, £1; Col. Weston, 10*s*.; Mr. A. Fitzgerald, 10*s*.; Mrs. Cunningham, 14*s*.; Col. Muter, 10*s*.; Rev. Mr. Usburne, 10*s*.; Mr. Samuels, 7*s*. 6*d*., and sundry sums of five shillings by Messrs. Thomas Knowles, Brand, Hignet, D. Gibb, J. Johnson, and the English Cricketers. By permission of the captain, F. Lillywhite, with the kind co-operation of the steward, also arranged a concert, to take place in the saloon, of which the following is a programme:—

SHIP IN DISTRESS—JIBBOOM LOST.

GRAND CONCERT, THIS EVENING, NOV. 8.

For the Benefit of Sailor, JOHN EVANS, who unfortunately had both legs broken during the gale of Saturday Morning, Nov. 5, while on duty.

PROGRAMME :—

Name.	*Song.*
Mr. REEVES...................	"Land Ho!"
Mr. SAMUELS	"Man, know thyself"—(was encored).
Mr. HOOPER	"Ever of Thee."
Mr. BARTON	(Accordion.)
Mr. CARPENTER..............	"Nothing More."
Mr. GRUNDY	"Paddy Whack" (was encored).
Mr. CAFFYN..................	"I have roamed o'er many Lands."
Mr. MOSES	"Good bye, Sweetheart, good bye."
Mr. JOHN LILLYWHITE	"We are Boys," &c. &c.
Mr. DIVER	"Love launched the Fairy Boat."
Mr. HARVEY	"Leonora"
Mr. FRED. LILLYWHITE	"Jolly Waggoners.'
Mr. M'BROOM................	"The Mermaid."

FINALE—"God save the Queen,"—by the entire Company.

S. S. *North Briton.*

The musical talents of Mr. Samuels and his brother performers were prominently brought forward, and were so highly appreciated that a considerable addition towards the total amount of the subscription was realized. Each of the officers and crew gave a day's pay, and some more. We find, in the ship's company, Mr. Cain, the experienced and attentive second mate, gave 10*s.*; Mr. Graham, chief officer, 5*s.*; Messrs. Naite and M'Donald, third and fourth mates, 5*s.* each; Mr. J. Bogg, carpenter, 5*s.*; Mr. W. Hatter, quarter-master, 5*s.*; Messrs. Gell and Ross, 5*s.* each. In the engineering department, Mr. Ross, the first engineer, contributed 10*s.*; the second, third, and fourth, as well as Mr. M'Dougal (boiler), 5*s.* each. In the steward's department, Mr. Newlands, the obliging purser, gave 10*s.*; Mr. Dolan, chief steward, 6*s.* 8*d.*; Mr. Watsen, 1st. cook, 5*s.* 4*d.*; and the remaining officers and crew, a day's pay. So far was the poor widow relieved, when the touching scene occurred of her coming to the ship's side to meet her husband on his return.

It was not until the arrival of the pilot on board that we were first informed of the dreadful disaster that had befallen the *Royal Charter,* and which intelligence created such universal consternation as to supersede the remembrance of our own hardships.

As we were in sight of the Liverpool lights we went aground, in attempting to come over the bar at the entrance of the Mersey, but fortunately that difficulty was soon surmounted by the energy of the captain, pilot, officers, and crew, and we landed on the wharf at Liverpool shortly before twelve o'clock, on Friday night, November 11, and three or four of the Cricketers were foremost in following the mail bags, and soon made their appearance at the George Hotel, after telegraphing to their respective families at home.

The distance we had travelled was as follows :—

	Miles.
London to Liverpool..........................	200
Liverpool to Quebec (not including going up the White Bay alluded to)	2,500
Quebec to Montreal............................	171
Montreal to New York........................	430
New York to Philadelphia........................	90
Philadelphia to Niagara Falls	450
The Falls to Hamilton........................	57
Hamilton to Rochester........................	210
Sunday's Trip to the Falls from Rochester......	140
Rochester to Rome...........................	145
Rome to Montreal............................	100
Montreal to Quebec..........................	171
Quebec to Liverpool..........................	2,500
Liverpool to London..........................	200
	7,364

Altogether, in round numbers, about 7,500 miles, from the 7th of September to November 11—a little more than two months.

Although the whole of the Cricketers have abundant reason to be satisfied with their trip, both as regards the treatment they met with at the hands of their American brethren and the triumphant results of their several matches, not to mention their pecuniary remuneration, which was was "*all*" they could expect, it is a very great question whether some of their number could be persuaded again to undergo the suffering and inconvenience consequent upon such a voyage.

The following will give a brief summary of the results of the five matches :—

Time and Place,	*Sides.*	*1st In.*	*2d In.*	*Total.*	*Result.*
September 24. Montreal.	Twenty-two.	85	63	148	England won by 8 wickets.
	Eleven	117	32	149	
October 3. Hoboken, New York.	Twenty-two.	38	54	92	England won in one innings and 64 runs.
	Eleven	156	—	156	
October 14. Philadelphia.	Twenty-two.	94	60	154	England won by 7 wickets.
	Eleven	126	29	155	
October 27. Hamilton, C.W.	Twenty-two.	66	53	119	England won by 10 wickets.
	Eleven	79	41	120	
Oct. 21.—Rochester, U.S. (the ext. match).	Twenty-two.	39	64	103	England won in one innings and 68 runs.
	Eleven	171	—	171	

By means of telegraphic despatches, and announcements by the "press," the British public were speedily apprized that the *North Briton* had arrived with her cargo, and by Saturday evening the Cricketers had safely reached their respective homes, but not until Grundy had sustained a slight detention by the custom-house authorities, who, evidently, were totally ignorant that they were detaining one who had just assisted, with others, in doing so much honor to his country. The circumstance, however, occasioned only a short delay, and arose from his being in possession of a little extra "weed," to enjoy by the fireside, whilst relating some of his American adventures.

THE DINNER AT GODALMING.

On Thursday, December 8, owing to the great interest that had been felt by the whole cricketing fraternity in the contests laid before the reader in this volume, and in which the native pluck and skill of our English players was put to the test, it was decided to celebrate the return of the Southern cricketers in a public manner, and to congratulate them upon the laurels they had won from their transatlantic rivals. A committee was accordingly appointed, under the management of Messrs. Challen, Colpas, and A. Whitbourne, who no sooner had placed a paper in the Public Hall, at Godalming, than it received the names of Henry Marshall, Esq. (the true lover and liberal supporter of the game, and the worthy President of the Surrey County Cricket Club), F. Yate, Esq., the Mayor ; H. Roker, Esq., Ed. Eager, Esq, Murray and Alex.

Marshall, Esqrs., &c. The President afterwards sent invitations to the following :—John and V. E. Walker, Esqrs., W. Burrup, Esq. (Hon. Sec. to the Surrey County Club), John Burrup, Esq., E. W. Napper, Esq.; as well as Wisden and John and Fred. Lillywhite (as Americans), the former, however, was unable to attend, owing to indisposition. The remainder of the Surrey Eleven were also invited, including Mortlock, T. Sewell, jun., Griffith, and J. Cæsar. F. P. Miller, Esq., was absent from unavoidable circumstances.

It is, perhaps, scarcely necessary to add, the four Surrey "cracks" were Lockyer, Caffyn, H. H. Stephenson, and Julius Cæsar.

The dinner took place at the Assembly Room, King's Arms, which was decorated in a very tasteful and appropriate style. The walls were adorned with laurel leaves and bannerets; on one side of the chair stood the Union Jack, and on the other the stars and stripes of the United States, whilst between them was placed a cleverly-executed design, star-shaped, composed of bats, balls, wickets, and other cricket accoutrements; across the centre of the room were suspended flags and festoons, interwreathed with the motto, "Welcome."

Upwards of 120 sat down, under the able presidency of Henry Marshall, Esq., Captain Alexander Marshall filling the vice-chair. After thanks for the repast, the Chairman rose and gave "the Queen, God bless her." (applause.)

In proposing "the Prince Consort, the Prince of Wales, and the rest of the Royal Family," the Chairman remarked that the Prince of Wales had joined a cricket club, and he hoped that his Royal Highness would become a member of the Surrey club (cheers.)

The Chairman next gave "the Army and Navy," observing that when they knew how brilliant were their achievements in other parts of the world, they might conceive of the bravery with which they would defend this land in case of invasion, aided as they would be by the militia and the gallant volunteers who were coming forward so readily in the service of their country (applause.)

The "health of the Bishop and Clergy of the Diocese" was then proposed by the Chairman, and he remarked that the Bishop supported cricket, and many of the clergy also favoured the game, and he wished some of them were present on that occasion (hear, hear.)

In giving "the Lord-Lieutenant and Magistrates of the County," the Chairman referred to the fact that many of the latter class belonged to their cricket clubs (applause).

The Chairman then requested the company to fill their glasses for a bumper, and proceeded to introduce the toast of the evening. He said—I have to propose to you the health of those gallant men who went across the Atlantic, in its most boisterous state, and travelled seven thousand five hundred miles, to exhibit to our American brethren the scientific, manly, and energetic game of cricket (applause.) After landing they had to take a long railway journey, and on their arrival in Canada they were received most generously. The next morning they had to enter the cricket field, and I expect were physically not quite in that comfortable state in which they had frequently entered the cricket fields in England. However, they conquered, and not the slightest jealousy was exhibited on the part of their brother subjects, the Canadians, but on the contrary, their welcome continued equally strong, and their departure was very much regretted. From Canada they went into the United States—to New York, where they were also generously received and hospitably entertained. Some allowance had to be made there for the rivalry which exists between the States and England, and it is not very surprising that the people who fancy they can speak English better than the inhabitants of this country themselves, should have expected that they were not much inferior in the game of cricket, and when they had such enormous odds as twenty-two to Eleven they had no doubt of victory. But the result was different; the English were successful as you know, and they won every match afterwards (cheers). They returned to England where their presence was most heartily welcomed. In America they had the opportunity not only of showing them good play, but also of seeing some of the greatest wonders of the world. Still, I am inclined to believe, they were extremely happy when they returned to Old England, and I do not think the comfort and institutions of this country have suffered much by comparison with those of the United States (applause). However I do trust that the very circumstance of going over there and cultivating a love for an object upon which both people can concentrate their attention, and which each had pleasure in looking at, will conduce to the existence of peace among us, and I do hope it will prevail (cheers.) If ever the Americans come to exhibit their prowess here, I am sure we shall receive them with all the delight becoming those who have one common origin, and show them all possible courtesy (hear, hear). I am confident that we, in common with all England, feel greatly indebted to those who went over to America, with the elements, in several instances, against them, and, under many disadvantages, sustained the honor of the country. We have met to thank them, and most heartily shall we thank them for the noble efforts they have put forth (cheers.) They have contributed to give the game a world-wide reputation, and now we ourselves must be careful to keep it up in all its integrity (hear, hear). I am sure you will have the greatest pleasure in drinking the health of the twelve cricketers who went to America (cheers.) In conclusion, I have to propose to you the health of the "Twelve Cricketers who went across the Atlantic," coupling with it the names of Messrs. Cæsar, Lockyer, Caffyn, Lillywhite, and Stephenson (drunk with immense applause.)

Mr. Julius Cæsar, after thanking the company for the compliment, said the twelve certainly had a very rough passage to America, but they did not care so very much about that. They landed at Montreal, and were rather disappointed to have to play the next day after their boisterous voyage ; however, they went into the field, but he could not say much about himself—the other ten won the game (laughter.) They certainly were received in Canada in a very kind manner ; but he could not say so much for the United States.* All he could say was, that they gained the five matches, and were proud of it ; not individually, but on account of the honour of their old country, (loud applause.)

---

* This remark, is considered, in the States, somewhat unjust, and perhaps, rightly so. Most of the twelve, we believe, were somewhat dissatisfied by the manner, *their Benefit Match* was managed here, and which appears the sole cause of the jealousy existing. *This was their own fault ; they should have looked after themselves.* But, says Cæsar, *the "United States !"* I thought the hospitality they received at New York, Philadelphia, and Rochester, was everything that a professional Cricketer *could desire*, as it was also in Canada, and many regretted that such words should have dropped from so renowned a cricketer as Julius Cæsar.—F. L.

Afterwards they were asked to play at base-ball, but as they had had no practice in that game, they refused to do so in less than twelve months. They passed into Canada again, and were wonderfully well received ; no people could be kinder than the Canadians, and he thought some of the twelve would have liked to have stopped on the other side of the Atlantic. They had a bad passage back, but all their troubles were as nothing to them when they met with the warm welcome which awaited their arrival at home, and he was quite sure there was not one of the party who did not love his old country now twenty thousand times better than ever (much cheering).

The Vice-Chairman then arose amidst great applause, and after referring to the importance of the toast with which he was entrusted, said : I should not be induced to enlarge upon the subject before me, were it not for the peculiar interest attaching to it, when we consider the high honour earned by this county, in producing so many of the representatives of the cricketers of England (cheers). I cannot but dwell with satisfaction upon the fact that this little county has afforded so large a quota to the champions who have taken part in the grand struggle. I am not so much surprised at the result, because I know that good stock will germinate and spread. It would be a source of wonderment to many to look into this room and see the company assembled ; I must say that I myself, with all my enthusiasm for cricket and knowledge of the love for the game which prevails in this neighbourhood, did not expect to find such a gathering—it shows only that the good old stock will come out (applause). Now that cricket has become popular, we see in these little towns the results of our early efforts in a great and noble and national cause (cheers). It rejoices me greatly to see how the long-expressed wish of my heart, that the game may be known in every country, is being realized. I helped to carry it beyond the Tweed, and I was one of the first to suggest that it should be introduced into Ireland. Now it has been taken across the Atlantic, and I have still another scheme to propose to you, and I hope you will follow it out (hear, hear). We have heard a great deal lately about invasions. Invasions ! I am not one of those who think anything of invasions. There have been several clever fellows suggesting sundry improved implements of war. Now

I have a little weapon of war to introduce to you. It is not a conical weapon or a cube, but it is spherical and made of leather, weighs five ounces and a quarter, and you can get it at Lillywhite's, Dark's, and many other places (laughter). It would do more for civilisation and the cultivation of good feeling than all the cannon balls in the world (cheers). Now I think, to make all meetings of a practical character, let us see what good may be disseminated from the journey to America. When the 12 players were there, some of them were very much pressed to remain; we could not spare them, but from the fact of their having been asked to stay abroad, we may learn how any one devoting himself to the scientific study of the game of cricket, may find a home and good remuneration (applause). Now I will mention my little proposition to you. Next year let us show how we can go with kind feeling towards another country close at hand, and take the eleven of England over to Paris, and I undertake to say we shall have as good a battle as was ever fought in the world (cheers). The French will get together their twenty-two, and after we have fought it out, let us finish it as we do in England, over a jolly dinner, and have some of the good blood of the country,—the only blood I ever wish to see drawn, some of their generous wine (applause). I have now to propose the health of the "Surrey Club," and to couple with it the name of one of the best fellows in the world, Mr. William Burrup, the Honorary Secretary (cheers).

Mr. Burrup, in responding, said it was always the object of those who managed the Surrey Club, to carry forward the game in such a spirit as would conduce, not only to its prosperity in their own county, but all over the kingdom, and he believed every member went into the field with a desire to promote the general interest of the sport (applause). He thought it was not needful, in a town which had been known to produce some of the best cricketers in Surrey. and had, in former years, contended with all England like Surrey had of late, to say what the county could and ought to do in support of the noble game (cheers). He trusted that for the future, the matches, with a list of which they would shortly be furnished, would be conducted in a creditable manner—cricket on the hearth as well as cricket on the heath was his motto (hear, hear). He hoped the club had not yet reached the pinnacle of its strength in members or ability, but that it would soon become a good battalion of a thousand strong (cheers). Mr. Burrup concluded by expressing the pleasure he felt in doing all he could for the good of the club and cricket in general, and by acknowledging the kindness and support of the members, by which he had been encouraged in many a difficult emergency (much applause).

The Chairman next gave "The Cricketers of Sussex," coupling with the toast the name of one of the best cricketers of the day, M Edwin Napper (cheers).

Mr. Napper returned thanks on behalf of the county of Sussex, and in an appropriate address he proceeded to propose the health of the president of the evening. He remarked that he was the first person who, when he (Mr. Napper) left school, took him into Kent to play his first match, and it was by his advice and teaching that he had gained a name as a cricketer. He was very pleased to find him now as the leader and the head of the Surrey players (cheers). He concluded by proposing the health of H. Marshall, Esq., and hoped he would long continue to enjoy good health to enable him to advance the interests of cricket.

Drunk with three times three.

The Chairman, in reply, thanked the company cordially for the honour done him. He said he had ever been an earnest supporter of cricket from his earliest days, and he could assure them that it would be his pleasure to continue that support to the utmost of his power (cheers). He had been elected president of the Surrey Club for one year, but year after year passed away, and they still continued to appoint him to that honourable post, so that he really thought it was time, at his advanced age, to withdraw (no, no). Well, he would assure them then, if it was their wish he would continue to fill that post, and he should ever exert all his abilities to further the important interests which the office involved (cheers). It would still be his desire to do this, and with the encouragement which their cheers afforded him, he would always be found ready, as before, to assist in every way the cause of cricket (cheers).

The Vice-chairman next gave "The Mayor and Corporation of

Godalming." The gentleman who filled the office of Mayor, he said, although not a cricketer, was always ready to give a helping hand to the cause of cricket (cheers).

Drunk with three times three.

F. Yate, Esq., (Mayor), responded, and in doing so extended a hearty welcome to the many influential friends of the cricketing world that he saw around him. He was sure it was an honor to the town to have their presence, and on behalf of the Corporation he returned them his hearty and cordial thanks for the flattering manner in which they had drunk their health.

F. Yate, Esq., then proposed "The Mayor and Corporation of Guildford," coupled with the name of W. E. Elkins, Esq. (cheers).

Mr. Elkins returned thanks on behalf of the Corporation of Guildford, and observed that he was pleased to find so many of the Guildford people present to welcome the return of the cricketers from the other side of the Atlantic, It was evidence of the universal good feeling of cricket, and it was gratifying also to find such kindly feeling manifested towards the Corporation of a neighbouring town, and for which he returned his most sincere thanks.

The Vice-Chairman next gave "The Visitors," coupled with a name which he said was a talisman to all cricketers in any part of the world —viz., John Walker, Esq. (Prolonged cheering.) He was personally known to the company present, for it would be remembered that some few years since, in this town, the three Walkers played against the three Cæsars; it was then that John Walker came in and performed an innings which won the admiration of all the cricketing fraternity. Mr. Walker's generosity was unbounded. His conduct proved that he valued deeds and not words, and his munificent assistance to the cause of cricket had never been equalled in any part of the world. (Hear, hear.) He would ask them, therefore, to fill their glasses and drink a bumper to John Walker.

Drunk with musical honours.

Mr. Walker, who was received with immense applause, rose and thanked the company for their kindness. They well knew his fondness for the game, and he could only express a hope that he might be long spared to show his love for the game. It would be a pleasure to him to see any of the company up at his house at any time, more especially when Southgate had to contend against England. (Laughter and cheers.)

Mr. Elkins gave "The Local Cricket Clubs," and expatiated upon their benefit in contributing to the Elevens of England. He coupled with the toast the name of Mr. Maddox, of the Chertsey Club.

Mr. Maddox acknowledged the compliment on behalf of the Chertsey Club, and said that although it was a small club, they could boast of having played 17 matches and only lost one. (Cheers.)

W. King, Esq., proposed the health of the Vice-Chairman, remarking that a better fellow than Alexander Marshall could not be found. (Loud cheers.) There was no man in the town more respected than he was. He was a sincere friend, an ardent cricketer, and a genuine friend of sport of all kinds. He (Mr. King) would express a hope that the townspeople may see a little more of him than of late, and he called upon them now to fill a bumper to his long health and happiness.

Drunk with musical honours and immense applause.

The Vice-Chairman replied in suitable terms, and observed that he could not understand why they should for one moment have doubted that he, Alexander Marshall, had been lost or wandered off the line, but, sportsmen as they were, they must know that an old fox will sometimes wander out. (Laughter and cheers.) He could assure them that whether it was in the hunting field or in the cricket field, his helping hand would ever be found ready to aid them. (Cheers.) He returned them his heartiest thanks for the high honour they had done him in drinking his health.

The Chairman proposed the health of the Dining Committee, joining with the toast the names of Mr. Colpus and Mr. S. Challen.

Mr. Colpus responded to the toast, and in doing so expressed a hope that during the season this year they should have the pleasure of seeing an Eleven of England in the town. He felt satisfied there would be little difficulty in finding the funds necessary for the purpose. (Hear.)

Mr. J. Burrup proposed the health of Frederick Lillywhite, whose exertions on behalf of cricket, in accompanying the Twelve to America, were worthy of their approbation, and also for his assistance in getting up the valuable statistics at the end of the cricketing season.

Drunk with three times three.

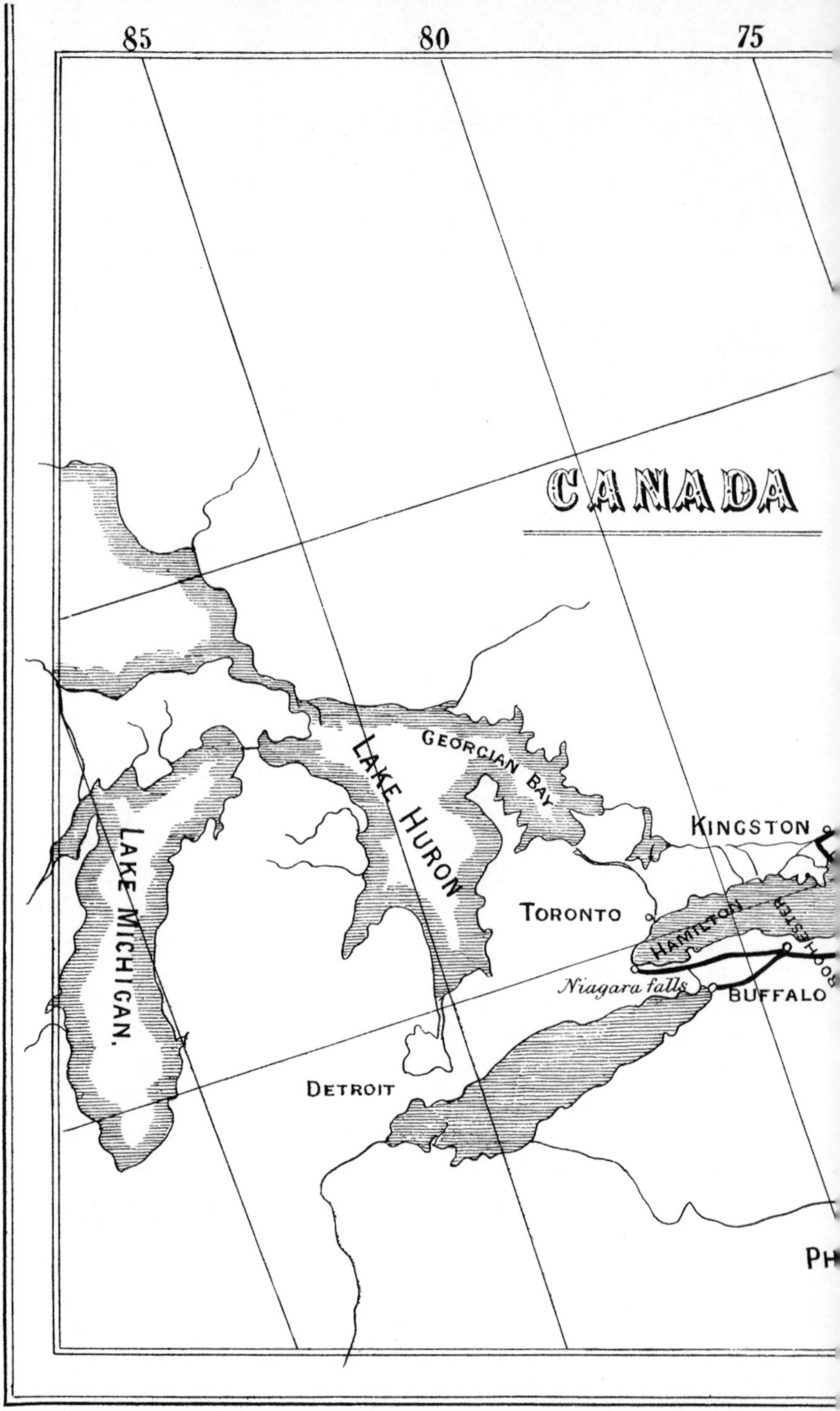

⁜ *This Bay was named by the Cricketers, the*

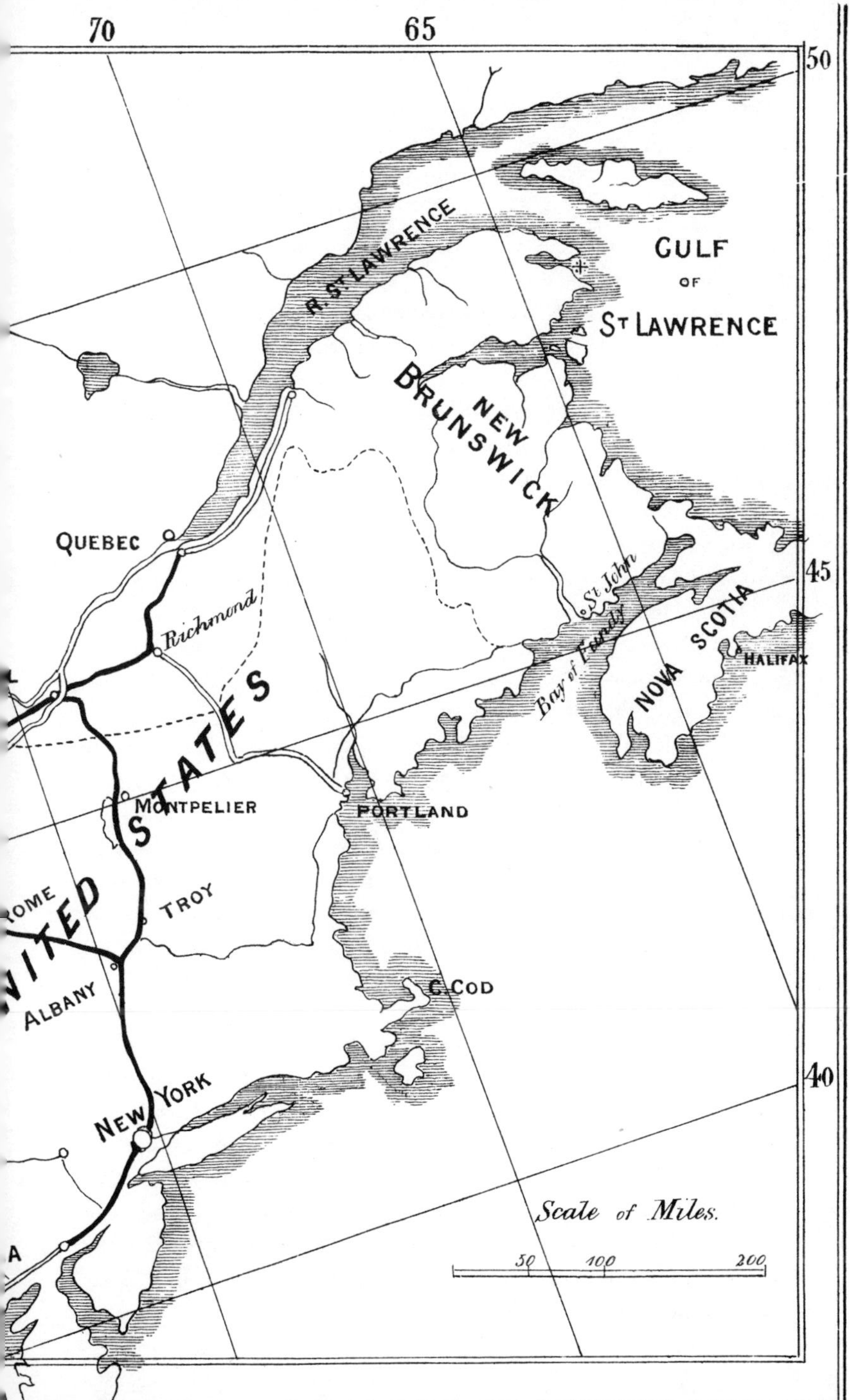

they having had a Sundays excursion by accident.

Mr. F. Lillywhite replied, expressing to the company his acknowledgments for the kindness he had experienced at the hands of the Messrs. Burrup—Mr. John Burrup, he said, being the foundation of the Surrey Club—and also from Mr. Pickering, of Montreal, and Mr. R. Waller, of New York, and, in fact, all the managers throughout Canada and the States. He alluded also to the fact of Messrs. Pickering and Baker affording all the assistance to him and the Twelve in their progress through their travels.

The Chairman proposed "The Press," coupled with the name of Mr. T. Chennell (*Surrey Times*), who briefly returned thanks,

Mr. Lyon gave "The Scorers and Umpires," coupling therewith the name of Mr. J. Baxter, who responded.

"The Ladies," the health of Mr. Cole, the host and a few other toasts, were given, after which the Chairman vacated his seat, and in leaving the room was greeted with deafening applause.

The harmony of the evening was greatly enhanced by the vocal services of Mr. Smith, of Caterham, and Mr. Bruton—the sporting songs of the former and the amusing ballads of the latter giving the utmost satisfaction to the company.

The pleasures of the evening were protracted to a very late hour; and thus liberally were the Southern part of the "Americans" treated; so much so, that they—Caffyn included—had by that time completely forgotten the hardships endured during the voyage. Two days' sporting over the Messrs. Marshall's estates finished the kind invitations to hospitable Godalming—a town that may be classed among those that have produced the "Fathers of Cricket," and where, and in its vicinity, many of the most influential supporters now reside.

We now, for the *finale*, lay before our readers a map of the country travelled through, obligingly furnished by Thomas Knowles, Esq., a fellow-passenger on our voyage home; and we conclude by stating that no assistance has been received, in publishing this work, from either of the managers of the "two celebrated Elevens," but that thanks are justly due to H. H. Stephenson, John Lillywhite, Diver, Lockyer, Grundy, Jackson, Julius Cæsar, Caffyn, Hayward, and Carpenter, all of whom, more or less, contributed towards the facts herein mentioned, and of which the compiler of them has the honor and pleasure of corroborating.

FRED. LILLYWHITE,

OF KENNINGTON OVAL, SURREY, LONDON, S.

The Compiler of "Lillywhite's Guide to Cricketers" begs most respectfully to inform Noblemen, Gentlemen, and Committees of the now numerous CRICKET CLUBS, that as soon as he has brought before the public his long looked-for work, "COLLECTION OF CRICKET SCORES FROM 1772," which will be (unless any unforeseen circumstances occur) in 1861, he will again enter into business at the West End of London, of which due notice will be given. His List of Prices will be considerably less than any other firm can possibly sell at, as F. L. will have advantages not to be attained by others. Being the promoter of supplying to CLUBS, &c., at WHOLESALE PRICES, when Manager of the firm of Lillywhite Brothers, also the late firm of Lillywhite and Wisden, Leicester Square, he can with the greatest confidence appeal to the Cricketing world for that support which he has for so many years received. All articles WILL BE MANUFACTURED under his own superintendence, and IMPROVED UPON, and none sold but what are genuine. He will have no connection with other firms, which he was the Promoter and Manager of since 1848. He can confidently state to the Cricketing Public of England, Ireland, Scotland, and Wales, as well as those of Canada and the United States, that no individual has had more experience of the MANUFACTURE OF ALL ARTICLES than himself, and he will, therefore, give his Patrons the benefit of that experience.

F. L. now supplies REGIMENTS, CLUBS, and SCHOOLS, &c., with LILLYWHITE'S REGISTERED SCORING BOOKS & SHEETS, &c., direct from Kennington Oval, and would, in the meantime, most respectfully caution the public from purchasing imitation sheets, which will not give members of a Club the necessary information when the season is concluded. They may be had in books for 50, 25, and 12 matches, price £1; 12s. 6d.; and 6s. 6d.; and 6d. a sheet. They will be sent *post free* on receipt of post-office order for the amount.

BELL'S LIFE IN LONDON "SCORE" SHEET, 2s. per dozen, post free, 2s. 1d. By the use of these Sheets (after the Score has been copied from the *Registered "Scoring" Sheet* at the conclusion of a match, and forwarded to the Editor of *Bell's Life*, 170, Strand) a notice of the contest will be inserted, which tends to make the game so remarkably popular. This sheet is also Registered for protection, as well as the SCORING SHEET for the securing of the analysis.

*** Piracy of these Registered Sheets is actionable, and the law will be enforced.